D0593131

The Book of Happy Endings

The Book of Happy Endings

True stories about finding love

Elise Valmorbida

Photographs

First published in 2007 by

Cyan Communications Limited
119 Wardour Street
London W1F 0UW
United Kingdom
T: +44 (0)20 7565 6120
sales@cyanbooks.com
www.cyanbooks.com

A CIP record for this book is available from the British Library

ISBN-13 978-1-905736-03-4
ISBN-10 1-905736-03-7

Typeset by Phoenix Photosetting, Lordswood, Chatham, Kent

Printed and bound in Great Britain by
TJ International Ltd, Padstow, Cornwall

Per Gregorio

~ ❦ ~

And for my mother
who taught me to read

Contents

FAST LUCK

FOLLOW ME

JINX REMOVING

EFUL HOME

JOHN THE
CONQUER

Fast Money
Blessing

Control

NE TO ME

ADAM+E

JOHN THE
CONQUEROR
Controlling
ADAM + EVE

DOMINATION
THE JUST
GAMBLERS

Go Away Evil
BLACK CAT
From
DO AS I SAY

Court Case

LOVE ME

I CAN YOU CAN'T

KEEP AWAY
ENEMIES
Road
Opener
HAND

7 AFRICAN
POWERS

Introduction

~ ❦ ~

And they lived happily ever after.

The romance industry thrives on froth and cliché, but that's not the kind of romance you'll find here. These are real stories about real humans who have a life to live 365 days of the year, not just on Valentine's Day. They are warm and vulnerable and idiosyncratic. Love is in the detail.

There is sorrow in these stories. There are questions, too, but no universal answers—no seven paths to a happy heart, or twelve steps to a perfect romance. (I'm always wary of numbered routes, unless they're in a road atlas.) But after I began writing this book, I did in fact come to a few general realizations …

Teenagers can't have happy endings

They're too young. They're fickle. You can't trust their emotions for a minute. Romeo, the archetypal young lover, is literally sick with infatuation. When he speaks about his feelings, it's half rant, half sonnet. He is obsessed, pining, lost to his friends. His love is a matter of life and death for him.

She is too fair, too wise; wisely too fair,
To merit bliss by making me despair:
She hath forsworn to love; and in that vow
Do I live dead that live to tell it now.

But this is not Juliet he's talking about! He's in love with Rosaline and can't function without her. Come to think of it, he might have enjoyed a happy ending if he'd been more constant in his affections and stuck with Rosaline—there wouldn't have been any of that Capulet vs Montague trouble. When Romeo turns up confessing that he didn't make it to his own bed the night before, Friar Lawrence says instantly: "God pardon sin! wast thou with Rosaline?" And Romeo replies:

With Rosaline, my ghostly father? no;
I have forgot that name, and that name's woe.

This sudden change of heart is all because he crashed a party and flirted with a dazzlingly beautiful stranger. It's significant that Juliet implores him to "swear not by the moon, the inconstant moon, that monthly changes in her circled orb, lest that thy love prove likewise variable". Shakespeare's hero is still learning the language of love and discovering himself through love. True to his name, he's roaming. Who knows if there's another beloved waiting in the wings? Who knows if R+J would have lived happily ever after?

Endings are only truly happy when they follow some quests and tests

There's no story if the princess never gets locked up, or lost in the wilderness, or paired off with a toad, or forced to turn heaps of straw into gold overnight. At the very least she has to wear shabby clothes for a while and do more than her fair share of housework. (This may sound like normal life to you and me, but she is a princess.) The paradigm works for princes and commoners, too. Happy endings feel happier after a bit of effort, or a lot. The people who take risks for love are inspiring. They dare to trust instinct, or strangers, and reveal their vulnerability. They have the courage to embrace change, perhaps upsetting others by doing so. They shut their eyes and jump into the void. They know it's easy to break something in a fall, and they can't possibly know if a happy ending awaits them or not. Besides, what makes an ending happy? There's a memorable bit of graffiti on a wall in East London: *It's never too late to have a happy childhood.* After meeting some of the people who appear in these stories, I began to think: *It's never too late to start a happy ending.*

Other people's happy endings make me feel happy

Most of these stories were told to me in personal interviews. It was a happy task prompting others to tell their tale. It was bizarre meeting total strangers in public places—blind dates!—asking very personal questions within minutes of shaking hands. It was a joyful experience, sometimes tearful. One couple described the storytelling process as cathartic. Another couple who pounced on the idea said instantly, "recalling how we fell in love makes us fall in love all over again". People delight in correcting each other, filling in the gaps of memory, hearing a personal revelation for the very first time (*You never!—I did!—You never told me!*), laughing at themselves and the things that used to worry them: shiny trousers, funny curtains, age difference, commitment ... their happy endings make me feel happy. If people who face the world with positive feelings tend to experience more positive events than those who don't, happy endings are better for you than spinach or chocolate. But this book is not about vapid happiness. There are unhappy endings out there—too many. And, I confess, there are unhappy endings in here. They lurk inside the wars, and the losses, and the farewells.

To make a beginning

Many of these stories open or close in London—a place I love because it's the world in one city. I'm interested in the journeys, the keepsakes, the way migration brings people together, tears them apart. Perhaps this is why so many of the lovers here talk about feeling at home with each other. A shifting notion of home is at the heart of who they are. It matters to feel at home. Or perhaps this is not just the talk of migrants. It's how people feel when they've crossed the island borders of self and discovered a new world with another person.

This book starts with research—friends and strangers, true stories heard or observed—and then metamorphoses into something like fiction. I have to say this, because *The Book of Happy Endings* is not a work of journalism or documentary reportage. Nor is it a collection of transcribed oral histories. I have faithfully quoted the words of others, but I have liberally used my own. I've put myself into people's shoes, tried to feel the weight of their luggage and see a story through their eyes. I've imagined scenes just as I do when I write about fictional characters, but I have never lost sight of the truth as it was told to me. Sometimes names and details have been changed to veil the identity of the individuals involved. Sometimes I'm present as the narrator-interviewer. At other times I've taken myself out of the picture altogether. Always I include my own subjective bias and feelings. Virginia Woolf recommended reading fiction, rather than memoirs or biographies, to find the truth about a writer's character. People have asked me why I don't include my own story here—*The Book of Happy Endings* is dedicated to the love of my life.

And finally …

My thanks to Pom Somkabcharti for first propositioning me and then accepting my formal proposal to write this book. Thanks to Anne, Jeanne, Greg, Steve, Aimee and Kelley for acting as literary go-betweens and match-makers. Thanks to Alma and Nadia for giving sound creative advice as good mothers and sisters do. Thanks to the 'love photographers' Augusto Braidotti, Rob Hann and Steve Mullins. Thanks to Tara Wynne for being my guardian agent. Thanks to the dedicated, opinionated chorus of Zenazzurrians: Anne Aylor, Aimee Hansen, Roger Levy, Steve Mullins, Annemarie Neary, Sally Ratcliffe and Richard Simmons. And big thanks the size of London to the lovers who trusted me with their stories. I can't acknowledge them here by name, but they know who they are. They told me their secrets. They showed me their archived messages, letters, treasured mementos and photographs. They shared their love with me. And, dear reader, they shared their love with you.

She was dear

It was 1946. Village Italy. Diletta's mother flung herself on the bed in tears.

It was a hard bed, and lumpy. The linen was darned and patched—they were saving up all their money.

They lived above the shop where they sold flour and semolina, dried beans and salt cod. Nice cheeses and hams were more plentiful these days. Sugar was still a luxury, but they sold it. Sugar had helped them survive the war. They'd sold it to the Nazis, to the partisans, to locals or foreigners, anyone who could pay for it. The customer was king. The real king had fled the throne with his tail between his short legs. Italy was ashamed.

Diletta's mother wept. Throughout the war, she had spilt not one speck of sugar. She had wrapped the precious sparkling crystals in rough paper, pinched and folded into makeshift packets. She had not wasted a scrap of anything, not allowed one morsel to escape. Never mind the King of Italy and Albania, the Emperor of Ethiopia. Never mind a daughter.

German soldiers no longer marched in, demanding special treatment. The place was full of Americans now. Food and animals. Different uniforms and different engines. Money. The prospect of renewal in amongst the destruction.

And destruction there was. All the bridges had been bombed. It didn't matter any more which side had released the detonators for what reason. The school had been blasted, the bell tower broken. Ransacked or ruined, stranded in waves of weeds, wild, the local villas were full of military personnel. The ancient quarries inside the hills had been filled with tanks and tents and arms. Barbed wire bound in a plot of maize or a vineyard. In a neighbour's field, men with parachutes gunned down from light-bleached night skies had been stripped of their watches, cloth, equipment. It didn't matter which side they were on. Just a few miles away, an avenue of pretty plane trees, unscathed and green again with healthy leaves, was now and forever a line of imaginary gallows. Everyone had seen the bodies hanged there by the Fascists, as an example.

Diletta's mother sobbed into the pillows, but not for the war. She and her family had survived that. She was aware that Domenica, the baby of the family, was standing by the bedroom door staring, sniffing, pitiful.

"Go outside and pick dandelion leaves for the salad!" Diletta's mother waved her off, before burying her head in the pillow and losing more tears.

Girls were a liability. How could a mother explain the weak-minded wilfulness of a daughter—to her husband Ercole, or to their first-born son Massimo, the next leader of the family? Girls were such a liability. Ercole would hit her for the shame. Women and children were like donkeys, he said, they had to be disciplined with a firm hand when they misbehaved. He was right. She had been too soft on her flighty daughter. She should have sent her to a house of correction. Perhaps it was not too late. Perhaps the Church could fix her. The priests knew how to fix wayward girls. What would Ercole say?

Diletta's mother wept into the sheets she had darned and patched and scrubbed in wood-ash water when there was no soap. With her strong arms she had stirred these sheets a hundred times in a giant soup of laundry. With her strong arms now she pummelled her wet pillow, beat the white parcel of chicken feathers that it was, plucked and stuffed with her own hands, better than straw. This was the bed where she had made love with Ercole, miscarried, lost blood and milk and water, given birth to slippery babies, thanking God the Father when they were sons.

She had apologized to her husband both times she'd produced a daughter. The naked sex of them had made her cry. It was Ercole who gave them their names. Diletta because she was dear. Domenica because she was born on a Sunday. Girls were a liability. He knew that, and she knew that. Girls cost money, got pregnant, gave away the family name. Girls were needy. She thanked the Holy Spirit for giving her more sons than daughters. Two boys for every girl. The arithmetic could have been worse.

Diletta's mother turned her head and looked up to the picture of the Holy Spirit on the wall, a kindly dove with small black eyes and rays of golden light all around Him, wings outstretched as if to take her into His feather-white embrace. It was the Holy Spirit who hovered above the Virgin Mary when the blessed fruit of her womb was announced. Diletta's mother thanked the Holy Spirit for her four sons, her sobs growing quieter. She cursed her daughters for the necessary mistakes in life that they were—like chickens and quails, she thought, their weak bones bending and breaking, their stupidity, their secrets, their endless production of eggs.

Diletta's mother sat up on her haunches, stroking the embroidered edge of the sheet, her own stitches. With God's blessing, the family had survived the war. They hadn't starved like some of their neighbours. Ercole and Massimo knew about politics, land, how to deal with officials, men in uniforms. And she herself knew how to treat customers. She had steered a neutral course between the hungry enemies and the hungry friends, because she knew that they could change sides at any instant, just like a treacherous mountain sky.

But children were always children. They had no choice. They had to take their parents' side. Blood was blood, steady as a millstone circling the same course, generation after generation. There was no dislodging it—

And now this.

They owned a couple of fields. They even had savings, coins and notes, in a secret tin—

And now this.

The whole family was going to emigrate, together, to the other side of the world where there was comfort. Safety. Money. Space. New things—

And now this.

Diletta had eloped. She'd secretly packed her girl's things and run away with a no-hoper, a man who had caught tuberculosis when he was fighting with the army. Vittorio was a foot soldier, a peasant. He came from a rough family. He was not old but he was already a war veteran. He was damaged goods. There wasn't a day of hard work left in him. Such a man would be no fit father, no husband to keep a woman and children through tough times. Not that Diletta was a woman yet. She was just a girl. The sin. The shame of it. What would the priests say?

Diletta's mother knew what Ercole would say.

Her husband would be mad as a bull in a black rage. He would disown his daughter, the infatuated girl with lipstick and powder on her face, and fashionable waves in her hair. He would ban her, shun her. At seventeen, she was too young to fly the coop, to be married without his consent. Too young to know she was underselling herself, discounting herself like inferior produce, setting a wicked example for her little sister. Too young to know that this no-hoper would only bring her down in the world. Diletta deserved better. The family deserved better. If they were to go anywhere, with the blessing of Jesus, the children would have to marry up in the world. Diletta's mother stared into the black dots of the Holy Spirit's bird-eyes. She crossed herself and prayed as tears streamed silently down her face.

Domenica appeared at the door again, her dress gathered up to hold the dandelion leaves she had picked, a heap of green tatters. Her little-girl legs were bruised and skinny. She was a sickly child.

"Your sister's run off with a ruffian!" Diletta's mother nearly spat the words, wiping the shameful tears off her eyes. "Get out of my sight. Go and play with the chickens."

I am sitting with Diletta in her open-plan kitchen living room. She lives less than a mile from her village bell tower. The TV is on, one talking head after another, jingling advertisements and showgirls, politicians on trial, murdered judges, news flashes. And food. Everything is hurried and jittery, except the food. Diletta glances at the screen occasionally. It's a source of background warmth and light, like an old wood-burning stove, flickering quietly on the inside.

The war is history now, but there are signs of it everywhere, not just the commemorative plaques and monuments. Not just the streets with famous dates for names. Black men from Ethiopia and Abyssinia come to Diletta's door selling statues and wallets, or looking for work. They speak African Italian. Albanians run rackets. Black women wait at quiet roundabouts and by cornfields, or totter along the roadside ditches, half-dressed for business. The shops in Diletta's village still provide for American soldiers, thanks to the permanent military base. Behind barbed wire, the quarried hills house nuclear missiles. Khaki-coloured trucks rumble along the narrow state roads. Bombers make test flights across the sky. Diletta receives a war widow's pension.

She has strong arms like her mother's, and big pink hands. She wears her wedding ring. She always does. It is sixty years since she ran away with Vittorio. There are still waves in her thick brown hair, and only a few grey strands she can count.

Today she has been working in her vegetable garden. She has been sowing seeds according to the moon—sow at the wrong time of the month and the plants will be weak and sickly, everyone knows that. She has pinched out her tomato plants, four different kinds in rows, nursed the fragile feelers of green beans along tall poles and wires, dug up baby potatoes and carrots, leaving others to grow, snipped sprigs of fresh herbs, lopped young artichoke heads off their spiky stalks. She has plucked out snails from the radicchio, lines of red frills and pale green, dark green ruffles of chard. She has cut a clump of lettuce for the salad. It's a long time since she's eaten dandelion leaves. She likes that bitter green taste, but lettuce is sweeter. There is so much food now, so much choice.

She has fed the chickens, walked through the clutter of their wings and squawks, repaired the fencing, gathered their spattered eggs.

She has washed the bed linen in her automatic washing machine. No need to boil and stir and scrub and mangle like her mother used to do. She has beaten rugs out of the back window. She has cleaned her floors until they shine in the strong rays of light that pour through the lace panels on her windows.

She has made pasta, draped soft sheets of it like calico over the backs of chairs, fed each strip through her press, laying out the tagliatelle ribbons in tangled nests to dry. The house smells of eggs and flour, soft and damp. There's also the delicious aroma of chicken stew laced with garlic and fresh herbs. She started cooking before the morning got too hot.

Diletta is a happy grandmother. She has pictures of her children, and her children's children. She whisks me through them, not lingering, not worrying about dates or places. This is her first-born's wedding, and these are the in-laws, good people. All the men had sideburns then, even the priest. This daughter of hers is a school teacher, a wise and patient woman with a big heart for children. This daughter-in-law is a teacher as well—she works too hard—they all do. This grandchild is grinning on a beach, summer sand and light in his hair. He's grown so much since then! This one is curled like a purring kitten over her gelato.

And this is Diletta herself with her family, posed together by a broken wall. She and her brother Massimo were teenagers then, quite sure of themselves in their Sunday best. Their younger brothers and little Domenica look poor and uncertain, heavy boots edged with dust.

This is the rest of the family after they emigrated, got married and started getting rich. It looks like a different world. Diletta didn't hear from them for a long time after they left.

And here is Vittorio, her husband, in black and white. He has a kindly face. Her parents had been right about one thing—God did take him early on account of his illness. He didn't live to give away his daughters. But he loved them as much as he loved his sons. He served his country. And he loved his wife. Diletta is not for one minute sorry that she married him, although she lived in widowed poverty for years, and the men who led her family shunned her for listening to her own heart and not theirs.

"And here, here's my father when he was young and in love." Diletta hands me an ancient brown-and-beige photograph. It has rippled edges like a seashell. I run my finger along the deckles. I look on the back. There are no names.

Ercole is a handsome man with dark intense eyes, a strong nose and a smooth, wide forehead. He's dressed up for the photo with a cravat and a rosette in his buttonhole, a white handkerchief folded carefully into the pocket of his jacket. He holds a walking cane, like a city gentleman, which of course he's not. It's a studio shot—behind him is a painted backdrop; the stick is a photographer's prop. Ercole gazes into his beloved's eyes. He is holding her hand. She is wearing a fur stole, a white frilled shirt tucked into a generous skirt that shows her straight slim ankles, and high-heeled dainty shoes. The image is surprisingly sensuous. I've seen wedding photos from this time and the couples hardly touch.

It takes me a while to realize that the woman standing next to Diletta's father, gazing into his eyes and holding his hand, is not his wife, is not Diletta's mother.

"Who is she?" I ask.

Diletta looks at me with a mischievous smile.

"His beloved," she says. "Look, here she is again."

Diletta hands me another portrait, dated 1920. There he is again, Diletta's father, this time seated, surrounded by four fresh-faced young women, all standing. The one on the left is 'his beloved'. She looks at the camera this time. Her eyes are dark and her hair is soft. Her skin is pale and there's a blush on her cheek. One hand is curled in a loose fist. The other holds Ercole's hand.

"Who are these other women?" I ask.

"His sisters, her friends."

Diletta sits back and waits.

I study the photograph. The women are all in pale shirts and dark skirts to their shins. In a half circle around Ercole, they are upright as guardian angels. They gaze steadily at the photographer's lens. There are no secrets here. He and his beloved are a couple. With friends and sisters they are a united front. They are being immortalized in black and white.

"So who is she? What happened to her?"

"She was a secret. We'd never even heard of her. But years later, long after my father and everyone emigrated, he came back to Italy on a trip. He was in his seventies then, but he was still fit and strong. He hadn't been back here for more than twenty years. The first thing he did was go up into the mountains and visit her."

"She's alive?"

"She was then. We found out that he'd gone to see this mysterious woman. He couldn't wait. We didn't know who she was. But she was the one he'd wanted to marry! She was beautiful, bright, vivacious. The love of his life."

"So why didn't he marry her?"

"His father forbade it, because she came from sickly stock. There was quite a lot of illness in her family. My grandfather wouldn't allow his son to marry a weak woman, someone who was going to be a liability. They thought she'd probably die young, or need looking after, instead of looking after him. It was all about survival in those days. And marriage was like a business. The funny thing is that this 'weak woman' had a long and healthy life—she ended up outliving all of them!"

"And Ercole just gave in?" I am thinking how this strong man with his defeated love had tried to defeat another love. But his girl had taken her own path. She had refused to make the same sacrifice. Despite the pressure. Despite the consequences. She had obeyed her heart.

Diletta nods. "He obeyed his parents. They said no. He submitted to their will."

Ercole had made his daughter pay the price for not being obedient like him.

"A bit later someone introduced him to my mother," Diletta says. "She came from a strong family, my word! Her mother was made of iron, she took against her sons' wives with a vengeance, drove two of them mad, one with melancholy, the other one died of TB, I think, or suicide. My mother was made of tough stuff."

"She must have known that she came second ...?"

"She was ambitious and hard-working, she never sat still or put her feet up, she was strong as an ox. And she had a bit of money. My grandparents approved of her. Ercole married her. They had us. They left Italy to start a new life with all the children—except me of course. I was with Vittorio. And my father left his beloved for ever. Until, of course, that visit, when he couldn't wait to see her after all those years."

"What was her name?"

Diletta smiles, as if she has been waiting for this question, like her secret at the heart of everything.

"Her name was Diletta," she says. "Same name as me."

New York, London

~ ❦ ~

Michèle lived with a roommate on the Upper West Side and worked in a music licensing company at Madison Ave and 43rd. She was two years out of college and hoping to make the most of her degree in Music and English. But it was a dead-end job. She was ready to quit.

One night, everyone from the office went out together. There was an English manager in town representing a European music library. He brought three English friends along. They stood together in the line outside the jazz club. They were skinny and un-American looking, but comfortable in their own styles, good to watch. It was the first time Michèle had seen guys rolling their own cigarettes.

Inside was dark and smoky, cramped and loud. At the bar, one of the English men flirted with a Danish woman. She was blonde and confident and wore striking horn-rimmed glasses.

Europeans are cool, Michèle thought. She had never been overseas, not ever.

A guy from work seemed to be interested in her all of a sudden, too interested. He leaned towards Michèle, monopolized the conversation. She wasn't really listening. He was nice enough, but not her type.

She didn't know what her type was.

Yes she did.

She had an unwritten list (she loved lists):

1. He wants to be with me Saturday nights, more than with anyone else.
2. I say what I want to say and he knows what I mean.
3. He respects women in general.
4. Intelligence.
5. Funny, but funny doesn't mean milk coming out of your nose.
6. Not tone-deaf; can't run the risk of tone-deaf kids.
7. Music. Art. Culture.
8. He has to love his family.
9. A liberal, open-minded outlook.
10. No religious nuts.

List or no list, she was tired from work, and thinking about going home.

Then one of the skinny English men sauntered up. His name was Marcus. He had on a cool shirt but he was wearing black shiny trousers which, now that she noticed them, bothered her. He'd taken off his flat cap. She saw that he had a buzz-cut and the beginnings of a bald patch, which was … honest. Nice eyes, big and blue. Freckles.

Michèle and Marcus started to talk. He was interesting, kind, intelligent, funny. He listened. He found her funny. She listened. He had grown up playing the piano and the oboe, he played guitar in a band and he'd set up a recording studio in his apartment—flat.

What a nice guy, she thought.

She liked the fact that he wasn't out to hook up. But he

wasn't her type either. She wasn't attracted to him, nor was she repulsed by him.

She noticed the pendant on a leather string around his neck. It was a rune, he explained, the symbol for justice. He was a lawyer. She asked if he was an ambulance-chaser. He found that amusing. He worked with juveniles in criminal defense and rehabilitation; one of his recent clients, a sixteen year old, had stolen an ambulance the very next day after his acquittal.

Michèle and Marcus talked for four hours, but she wasn't counting.

"What are you doing after this?" he asked.

"I've gotta work tomorrow," she said.

"We're going to Automaton. You're welcome to come along."

Michèle knew from the club's name that she would not like it. She hated techno computer music. It was insufferably dull. For her, music mattered, and it had to be human.

"I need some cash," she said. It was true, but it was also an excuse.

"I can lend you some," Marcus said.

She couldn't tell if he was just being polite.

"Lemme get some money," she said. "I think there's a bank machine down the road." She was too cowardly to say that she was going home.

Outside, she looked and failed to find a money-mover, then she tried to hail a cab. It was after midnight and there were people everywhere, but there was not one free taxi in the Village, or in the island of Manhattan. Soon there were no taxis at all in the entire city of New York. She started to feel alone and nervous.

Marcus appeared outside the front door of the jazz club. He seemed to be looking for someone, perhaps for her.

Michèle crouched down and hid behind a parked car. What was she going to do? She'd been caught out trying to escape. She stayed there, squatting, until she could bear it no longer.

This is a farce, she thought, and stood up. She felt like a girl in a cake, or a clown.

He waved when he saw her.

"I can't find an ATM," she said to him, crossing the street.

"Don't worry, I'll sub you."

He lent her $20.

It took them no time at all to find a cab. Not one solitary minute.

Automaton was worse than she'd imagined. A hot, smoky, sweaty basement flashing with strobe lights. Music that thumped in her ears, grated. The antidote to dancing. Michèle drank a half-hearted beer and half-danced. Marcus was full of energy, exuberant and attractive, but Michèle thought: *if this guy likes this kind of music, I don't know if I can even be his friend.* It was 2.30am and she was tired. She worried about work the next day.

"I've gotta go home," she said at last.

"Let's call it a night then," Marcus said. He rounded up the others.

It took them no time at all to find a cab, Michèle couldn't help but notice. Marcus sat in the back with his English friend and the Danish blonde (she of the horn-rimmed glasses). Michèle sat in the front and talked to the cabbie all the way.

When they arrived at her apartment block, Marcus passed Michèle a slip of paper with his address and telephone number. She handed him her business card.

He jumped out of the cab and gave her a double-cheek kiss, so un-American.

"I'm leaving tomorrow," he said. "It was lovely meeting you."

"I owe you $20," Michèle said.

As she went up the sidewalk to her door, she thought: *what a shame he's leaving*. The thought surprised her.

Garden of love

Pani is twenty-eight years old, slight and girlish. Her complexion is pale and her hair is long and black. Her eyes are big and wide, dark as coffee. She has never learned to whistle, and it bothers her when she thinks of it, but she has learned many other things. She has learned to fall in and out of love. She is single now and she doesn't mind too much. She has English as a third fluent language, after Swedish (her best) and Persian (her first). A degree in marketing from the USA. A year of work in Tehrangeles, the capital of California, otherwise known as LA, where she learned to live without her family. That was a hard lesson in solitude, despite the comfort of cousins and friends, and she felt the ache of longing. Then she moved to England for her MA and learned the joy of being reunited: her whole family joined her from Sweden in their second life migration. They live in London now: Pani and her mother, father and younger sister.

Tonight she has been out for the evening with friends. She's looking into the bathroom mirror and washing off her make-up. She hears the phone ring. It's after ten o'clock, rather late. She hears her mother go to the phone and pick it up. Her mother sounds animated as she talks to the mysterious caller. She's speaking Persian, not Swedish or English. Pani wanders out of the bathroom, curious.

"It's an old friend," her mother whispers, shielding the handset. She talks some more about their life in London and then her voice changes. She passes the phone to Pani. "Say hello."

"Hello," says the telephone voice, in English.

"Hello, this is Pani. To whom am I speaking?"

"You sound grown up," says the voice. "Don't you recognize me?"

"Give me a clue," says Pani.

"It's Ali from Germany. The happy person from the north."

It is the translation of his name. Pani is speechless.

Ali says: "My dad was in Tehran and called your grandmother. He couldn't believe his ears when *your* dad answered the phone."

"He's over there for work. What a coincidence!" Pani is looking wide-eyed at her mother. "Do you live in Germany now?" she says into the phone.

"Yes, well, I should say *lived*. Near Stuttgart, where the people are very stiff and honest and in your face. We would have been happier in France. They take their time cooking. *Savoir vivre*. More like us. But I'm in England now. I'm setting up a company with my brother."

"Here?"

"Yes, we're both here now, in London. Hey, do you want to meet up?"

He sounds nice, but it's difficult to judge with men. One has to meet them and see how they behave. Pani gives him her mobile phone number. She's being polite to overcome her amazement. Her mother is looking pleased.

"When did you leave Iran?" she asks.

"I was eight," Ali says. "We spent a year in Switzerland first. I wasn't too happy there. The best part of my childhood was already over. Then the war ended. And we moved to Germany, where the people are very stiff and straightforward and … not like us. Mum and dad are both settled there though."

Pani remembers Ali's mother and father. She pictures them at her house, enjoying good meals with her family, listening to music, applying sun-tan lotion by the pool. She remembers one day in particular.

Pani is eight and a half years old. She has a dark brown shiny mop of hair, cut like a boy's, a lean body tanned to gold by the summer sun, big eyes dark as chocolate. She lives in the best part of town, Shemiran, north of Tehran.

It is 1986, a lovely hot August full of swimming and playing and parties. The war with Iraq has been going on for six years now, although she can't be absolutely sure. She was so very little when it started. She doesn't know much about the war, because her parents don't discuss it. But she knows that during the worst bombings there was a blackout, and she had to hide with her little sister in the closet. They played in the dark with their dolls (the ones their mother hadn't yet sold) to pretend that nothing bad was happening.

Don't tell people at school we're selling things, Pani's mother keeps saying. It is a secret.

Pani loves her mother. She can't imagine loving a mother any more than she does. Her mother is a dentist, a strong and clever woman with lots of friends. Everyone says she comes from a long line of strong mothers. Pani loves her father too. He is very handsome, and an architect. Both her parents make money, which is why they live in the best part of town. They have drinks and dinners and barbeques by the pools—there are two swimming pools, one for the grown-ups and one for the children. They don't have to worry about making noise. They have music, which troubles the Revolutionary Guard, but the trouble can be fixed with bribes. They even have musicians. And they have alcohol. They can make as much noise as they like because the neighbours on either side have moved away. (They were friendly with the Shah.) The whole street feels empty now. Nearly everyone seems to have moved away.

Sometimes Pani stares at the mountains—she can see the Damavand peak from her house at the edge of the empty, dusty land—and she wonders if that's where people go. In winter the mountain looks like a white satin skirt held out for a curtsy. In legends Zahak the dragon-king was slain there. At school Pani learns that the peak is more than 5,000 metres high. She likes numbers. She has the measure of things. Her garden is 10,000 square metres within its tall walls. After the sliding doors of the house, there is the white marble patio with the yellow plastic awning casting a lemon light upon the whiteness. Then there are the two swimming pools surrounded by roses, so many roses, too many to count. Pani is addicted to their intense perfumes, each one different, and their colours: mauve silk, apricot velvet, shell pink, ivory white, crimson damask. Then there are the fruit trees. Since spring, Pani has been watching the bee-filled blossoms turn to green buds turn to shiny-bright cherries and plump pears. Even on these hot days, when the temperatures reach past forty degrees, she finds coolness in the green shade of the trees. Her garden is like the gardens in her storybooks, like Eden.

"Come and see what the robbers left behind," Pani whispers to Ali, so that the other children and the grown-ups can't hear. Ali is seven years old, a year and a half younger. They are inside the house. There have been lots of robberies. This time the burglars were glimpsed climbing in through the window.

Pani's parents and Ali's parents are great friends. Pani's father the architect works with Ali's father the business man. They have a company together. Their families do everything together. Holidays by the Caspian Sea. Picnics. Birthday parties. Pani can't remember a time when she didn't know Ali and his brother.

"Come and see what the robbers left behind!" Pani leads Ali out through the sliding doors. "It's really weird."

He follows her out to the patio beneath the lemon awnings. He is her best friend. He can whistle and it makes her jealous because she can't whistle to save her life, despite hours and hours of practising.

She takes him to where the guard dog has left its droppings. She knows, secretly, that it has nothing to do with the robbers but, ever since the secret selling of things, and the blackout, and the recent burglary, she can sense adventure in the air. She takes Ali by the hand and they stand together in the quiet heat.

He looks at her in a special way and then he kisses her on the mouth. He is her best friend, but they have never done this before. She kisses him. This is her first kiss. Ever. She knows it is naughty. Like being grown-up. She doesn't stop. He doesn't stop. It feels like a secret adventure.

A few weeks later, Pani's mother is taking the whole family to Sweden for a dentists' conference. They spend some time in Frankfurt, which is fun because they go to the zoo and eat German hot dogs, and Pani has never been to Europe before. They arrive in Stockholm airport with their holiday luggage and the guard looks at the visa belonging to Pani's mother.

"This dentists' conference is over," he says. "The dates have passed."

That's when Pani's mother says that they have run away from Iran because of the war and they would like to live in Sweden. So they do.

Pani goes to school. It's different from school in Iran. It's not religious. She doesn't have to listen to the single voice praying and praying every morning. She and the other children don't have to shout *Down with USA! Down with Russia! Down with England!* at the start of the day. She doesn't have to wear the grey *maghnae* headscarf and *rupush* jacket. The boys and girls are mixed up together. They all seem to be blonde, except for Pani. She learns Swedish but she doesn't learn how to whistle. She forgets about Ali, even though he was her best friend and they never did say goodbye. She grows up.

Pani shows me a photograph of all the children dressed in their finest for a birthday. Lined up with their favourite friends and cousins, Pani and her sister wore matching long white dresses, with puffed sleeves and frills of tulle over satin underskirts. They both looked like princess dolls, even though Pani's haircut was boyish. Ali was wearing a Starsky & Hutch top with brown leather patches on the shoulders and elbows. His little hand rested on Pani's knee.

There is another photo of them all together in a bright yellow dinghy, bobbing about on chlorine-blue water. Squinting in strong sunlight. Ali was looking at the camera, reaching back, holding Pani's hand.

"Look at my hand in each photo," Ali says. "I loved her even then."

"He can't have been older than six!" Pani laughs. "He's a giant now, look at him. The first time he called my mobile, he left a voicemail, and I passed the phone to my sister so she could hear. His voice is very nice. I told her: *he's very sexy*. That was before I saw him again. I invited him over for lunch. He came along with his brother. I opened the door and greeted them. I thought: *oh my god, they're both so handsome, I can't believe it*. I knew they'd be tall. Our mothers had confirmed the details!"

Ali strokes Pani's hand. "My mother asked her directly on the phone, she said: *are you tall?*"

"I had to say I'm not." Pani shrugs.

Ali looks at her as if to say she is the perfect size, as if he could look at her for ever and it would not be enough.

"We spent the evening together," says Pani.

"I felt so at home, so comfortable, after all these years."

"He was giving me compliments all night, in Persian, in English. In front of my mum! I thought that was quite cheeky of him. He said I had beautiful hands."

"You were doing your nail polish in front of us!"

Pani grins. "We went out together, just the two brothers and the two sisters."

"We had the best drinks. Pimm's and soda. The first time I'd tried it." Ali keeps stroking her hand. "The best drinks."

"When he got tipsy he said to me: *do you remember that day?*"

"And she pretended not to know what I was talking about!"

"I was embarrassed. I said *let's not talk about it now.*"

"And I said to my brother: that's my first girlfriend."

"Our mothers are very good friends again after twenty years apart. They keep asking us: *are you together?* They keep prodding, trying to get me to say things, but it's still early days and we want it to be free like any other love, without pressure."

"They don't know," says Ali. "It's our secret for now."

"Women know!" Pani laughs. "Don't fool yourself that they don't know. You might not admit that the sun exists, but it exists anyway."

Love libraries

~ ♡ ~

Declan notices the head librarian. There is something about her manner, her movement, that catches his attention. She writes at her desk. Left-handed. She scrawls strangely.

"I'm left-handed too," Declan says in English. His Lithuanian is still poor, enough to get by and be polite. He can't quite face the idea of sitting down with a pile of language books. Lithuanian is difficult and complicated. Even the local teenagers say so.

The head librarian looks at Declan and smiles a quiet, closed smile. Declan has decided that all Lithuanians are reserved. Turned in on themselves like houses with shutters against storms. They open up with beer and vodka. The Russians here are much more confident. They come from a big country. They're gregarious and proud.

The head librarian talks a little. It's hardly banter. Her English is very good. The old Soviet system did not approve of left-handed writing, so the suppressed script escapes every which way from the pressure of fingers.

Declan grew up in the late capitalist West, where

children were encouraged to express themselves so freely that their wayward scrawls compete with any Soviet left hand.

The head librarian smiles politely again.

Declan goes. He is feeling melancholic. He's alone in a port by the Baltic Sea. It's just a couple of months until Christmas and the weather is unnaturally warm, degrees above zero, not much snow, an Indian summer. How is he going to survive the festive, restive season? Christmas is a family event but all his family are back home in Ireland.

It is late. Declan returns to his flat and prepares for his next class. His Lithuanian home is heated by state-owned boilers that turn on automatically when the temperatures dip. Declan spends his days and nights teaching English as a second language. He needs to manage a few jobs to make ends meet. He has a one-year contract to teach office workers at a shipping company, every day during their lunch hour, early before their working day and late after the offices close. He fills their downtime with proper nouns, possessive articles, irregular verbs, the active and the passive voice. He has another contract, with a mobile phone company, evening classes. Another with a travel company. And private students, lots of teenagers doing English at school.

Friday is his one day off.

He's in the supermarket, stocking up for the week ahead. Christmas looms. Soon it will be taking over the shelves just as it does back home. Declan sees the head librarian again. She looks pretty, but not in a conspicuous way. He thinks he will ask her out, but for now he knows to keep his distance. There is something guarded about her and he can feel it. Besides, he's not looking for love. He says hello. She is polite and friendly. Her name is Rasa.

Another Friday, he goes to the jazz bar opposite his flat. People assume he's rich because he's foreign. It's easy to pick up girls and have a good time, he knows it. It's a kind of misplaced glamour, the power of the stranger in a poor place. Declan sees Rasa there, with friends. A matter of chance, but the chances are greater in a small city. They greet each other.

Most of the other women are dressed up like dolls. Heavy make-up and long nails. But Rasa is more understated. She is stylish, smart, natural. She is thinking about how easy it is for foreign men to pick up girls here and have a good time—Declan knows it. Rasa is not that kind of person—Declan knows this too.

They share beer and vodka snacks, delicious bread with garlic, fried fish, chickpeas, salami, fresh food to go with endless drinks. Rasa has a sense of humour and a quiet, strong way about her. She's intelligent. Interested in the world. Her blue-green eyes are sad, but her smile is not. Her name means falling dew.

Declan asks her out. He's tentative.

Their first date is not obviously romantic. They meet at a pizza place near the railway station in the middle of the afternoon, to fit between their shifts. The conversation is casual and general. They talk about Lithuania and work and weather. They get on. Maybe that's all they will ever do.

Declan walks her to the bus stop. A long way. It rains and rains. They've come unprepared, no raincoat, no umbrella. They're both drenched. The rain releases their laughter.

They meet again, but it's not intimate. They go to the cinema. They wait for the film to start.

Declan says: "I think you're really nice."

Rasa says: "I'm nothing special." It's not a lament, more a statement.

Eventually she tells him she's been through a difficult divorce and has two children. She spends most of her free time with them. She went out to the jazz bar because she had friends visiting from Vilnius. Her husband left her for another woman. She's had to move back into her mother's house and her brother is an alcoholic. She does not want love or pain.

Declan meets her children. They go to the beach one day, all together. The girls think it's funny that he speaks English. They are both curious and suspicious of him, a little possessive of their mother. The beach is lovely. Rasa too.

When the snow arrives in December, Declan asks her to join him for New Year's Eve. It's a bold move. He doesn't know how she'll respond. It matters. They sit in a bar and gaze through glass as the town square turns softly white in the night. She accepts his invitation. They start the new year together, drinking champagne and watching fireworks from his window. She stays the night.

The relationship slowly, unsurely, feels more real. Declan wonders if he can deal with her pain. He doesn't know if there's a chance to build something new with Rasa. The women at work start asking her: *Is it love? When is he going to leave? When will he go back home?*

Back home, Declan had lived with his dad in a council flat, until the old man died. Here was the son with no career, no money, no partner, and now not even an ailing father to care for. At least he had a home. And a part-time job as a counsellor for a local charity. His work was unpaid.

What was he to do with his life? He'd thought about teaching English as a second language, but all the courses were unaffordable, thousands and thousands of pounds. He had no savings. He was on the dole. Nobody was going to lend him money. He wanted to change his life but somehow everything depended on something else.

At his local library, Declan saw a poster advertising grant-assisted places for TEFL training. To pass the aptitude test, he needed to master grammar—something that his modern comprehensive schooling had neglected. So he returned to the library, day after day, to study. Proper nouns, possessive articles, irregular verbs, the active and the passive voice. He was his own teacher and he found it very difficult being his student. He passed the test but didn't get any further. The courses were over-subscribed. He was competing against graduates with degrees in English, languages, linguistics. His disappointment was paralyzing. He wondered if his luck would ever change. It did. One day the phone rang.

"Someone has dropped out," the voice said. "I've been looking through the applications. I've called you on the off-chance. Can you start now, today?" She transferred the grant over to his name so that he would have all the books and materials he needed to do the course. It was the kindness of a stranger.

When Declan graduated, he knew more than he could learn from library books. An inspiring teacher had told him: “What you do in this work is bring out your personality. If you can express yourself, you can do the job.” He had learned to do just that. He was moving from the passive to the active.

He worked hard at an English language school that closed down suddenly and didn’t pay his wages. Then he took up a teaching position in a small industrial Slovakian town near the Ukraine border. He drank to keep warm but he nearly died of cold and loneliness. His bank card was stolen by criminals. He left after three months, disappointed at his own naivety. He taught over the summer in London, before moving to Czechoslovakia where he taught for a year in poor conditions, badly paid.

Too many irregular verbs.

And then he found work in Lithuania, where the grammar is complicated and the people are reserved.

He found another library.

Snow, rain, falling dew.

“Is it love?” he asks.

He answers his own question. He’s not thinking about getting a job anywhere else. He’s in love. He’s very fond of her. He admires the way she copes, the way she works hard to manage her troubles, everything. Expressing emotion is not so easy. Things are not always clear. He has to remind himself that English is not her first language. Expressing emotion can be difficult even when the words are familiar.

“But we can just go out and not have to talk and we feel comfortable. That’s love. And I can’t picture it ending.”

New York, London II

~ ♡ ~

Dear Michèle

I'm back in England full of the images of an incredible week in your city—the vibrancy, the energy, the friendliness are all echoing around my head and the grey skies here seem fitting and symbolic.

Thank you for making my last night in New York such a good one. I enjoyed talking with you and your qualities reflect those of the city. I hope the Friday was not too unbearable for you—I heard you were a little worse off for it—I hope you felt it was worth it!

I seem to remember saying I'd send you some of my musical efforts. You'll see two tracks on the CD. They are very old now—I recorded them over a year ago and feel I have moved on since. The tape has some more recent stuff. I'd be interested in your comments.

I hope your gigs went well. I really miss playing live. It can be such a good buzz. I think I'm too studio-based and need to get out a bit more! Perhaps I'll pick up my guitar again and find a band!

I've been thinking hard about moving out of England. I worry that my week in New York was like a holiday romance—exciting and intense—but unsustainable—that I'm looking at everything in an unrealistic way. I came back and had to go to a company dinner thing and was back among all the people that I work with. They have offered me a partnership and I really have to decide on whether I want to be locked in there like a clipped bird for however many years. There's got to be more than financial stability to existence?

I don't know why I'm writing this to you actually—it's really not your concern! Perhaps some connection with another way/side is what I need, writing blindly to someone I met for a few hours and shared some thoughts—unconnected with the usual scheme of existence—whatever—it feels quite good!

I hope you find happiness and success through your music. I think maybe you need to be doing creative things—you seem to have so much energy and vitality to give. I think the most important thing is to express what comes really from inside you—what you really feel and think rather than what seems most fashionable. If it hasn't come from the heart it will always sound hollow and disposable—like most pop music—I'm guilty of doing it, as is everyone, but the best stuff always shines through with real honesty.

Michèle, I really hope you like the music. It was wonderful to meet you. You have made a strong impression on me. It would be good to meet again somewhere, sometime. You're always welcome here.

Love
Marcus
xx

Hello, Marcus ...

What a pleasure to receive a package from my long lost British friend! I was folding laundry in my living room last night (yes, I lead an exciting life) and my doorman buzzed up that I had a delivery, so I ran downstairs wondering what it could be.

I was surprised, but that doesn't mean I'd forgotten about you. In fact, I've thought of you frequently since our evening a few weeks ago. I so enjoyed just talking (dancing, laughing) with you. It's rare that I spend time with a guy I've just met and not sense an ulterior motive.

The night you flew back home a bunch of us went out again, but I was so incredibly exhausted that I left the restaurant with apologies all around. I was going on three hours of sleep. It's funny, because that used to be my lifestyle. My last two years of college I played three or four nights a week, mostly out of town, and I'd still have to make it to class in the morning after not getting to sleep until 3 or 4am. It was so completely normal for me then, but once I started this job my schedule got changed all around and now I find my eyelids drooping at 11pm.

I'll be leaving this job in the next few weeks. I'm so terribly bored. I really need to get a waitressing job at night so my days are free to audition full time. I plan to give my notice next week. I apologize if this letter seems impersonal what with typing and all, but my handwriting is fairly disgusting. Besides, I can write a lot more and a lot faster on the computer.

Incidentally, your handwriting is lovely.

My gig went well. I felt good about the night, but

there seems to be a problem with the pianist. See, the music is all his, so basically he's a solo artist with a back-up band. It isn't like we're a duo, even though my voice is featured (his choice). At the risk of sounding conceited, much of the crowd was there for me, and most of the applause was aimed in my direction. That seemed to bother him. But hey, he picked me. I have a feeling he may kick me out at some point. But that's OK.

I enjoyed your music. I'm flattered that you sent it to me. I must be honest with you and say that I'm normally not one to throw that kind of music into my CD player, but because it was yours I felt a more personal connection to it. I liked what you did rhythmically and how each instrument, or sound, gradually developed into something else every few minutes. I had to really pay attention and follow the line of it all.

I really get inside music. It surrounds my head so that I can almost see the music. Does that make sense? I've explained it to people that way before and most have no idea what I mean. I can't explain it any better.

So I guess you won't be moving to NY. How could you turn down a partnership? I do understand your predicament. You don't want to base your decision on a week of partying, yet you don't want to base it on the security of a place you've lived your whole life, either. You must ask yourself, will I get the opportunity to live in NY (or any other foreign city) again? And unfortunately money does matter a great deal, as much as we'd like to claim it doesn't. Is your NY job still being offered to you? Are they holding it for you? How long do you have to decide?

I imagine NY looks a lot like London right now. The

last few days have been rainy and in the low 60s. I like it, though. The mist on my face makes me feel clean and refreshed. I feel like I'm in some old romantic city (which I guess I am). I just don't want it to get cold too quickly!

As far as your potential move goes, make a list of the things you'd be missing out on if you moved and then a list of the things you'd be missing out on if you stayed. Do it for both cities, and base your decision on which list has the most positives. I know that sounds corny and simple, but man, I live my life by lists. I'd never remember a damn thing or get anything done if I didn't.

I appreciate your spelling my name right. Not only did you get the direction of the accent, but you placed it over the proper 'e', something most people don't do. My assistant repeatedly uses an apostrophe! Whatever.

I'm happy to hear you were as affected by me as I was by you. It was a pleasure, Marcus, and I hope that, regardless of whether you move to the States or not, we can continue our correspondence. If I can afford it, you can be sure I'll take a trip to England ('if' being the operative word). Keep me posted as to what your decision will be. I do so hope you return to NY sometime soon, as I'd love to pick up where we left off.

Where was that, exactly? Oh yeah, I was talking our cabbie's ear off.

Take care, and thanks again for your wonderful letter. Write again …

Love,
Michèle

Dear Michèle,

At last I can sit on my sofa at home, relax, get out some paper and a pen and write back to you. It's 11pm and I've just finished a one-hour telephone conversation about a court case for Friday. It's all very intense and getting nowhere. I hope by writing I can take myself out of all this and dream of better times and places!

It was good to hear from you. I really enjoyed your letter—it read as I remember you spoke—sharp and vital and full of good healthy US expressions! I was pleased and excited to hear from you.

I'm still feeling strong feelings about moving to your town. The job is there for me, but it depends on the organization getting some funding, which they hope to get soon. It wouldn't be legal work, but it would be youth work, which is sort of what I do anyway. I like the lists idea. It is hard to categorize a gut feeling—although I guess that goes into the list too. I have this feeling it is going to happen. Everything seems so grey here now. My friends are always good for me but I'm sure they'd spend most of their time in NY if I went there!

I'd like to hear your voice—if you've got any basic tapes of your voice send them over—I can sample them and do some dance remixes!! You probably think that is sacrilege. I understood what you said about music as being a surround thing. Sometimes I draw pictures of the way a song should feel—if you picture it and even represent it with colour and lines as you keep hearing it, you can see if you are still true to the original idea.

I live for music. I play it all the time. When I get

home I crank up some booming house beats. In the car I'll travel to all sorts of stuff. I think it gives you escape but also gets you to think about what's going on—how a lyric can hit home and make you think—too often however I think people don't try with words—they are all effect without depth. This is why I got into dance music (apart from just getting lost in it, letting go). It just ignores the idea of a song in favour of effect. I don't think it appeals to the intellect at all—it is just sensual.

I think we need a balance of both—ideas/thoughts and sensual feeling.

I don't write many letters. It's quite strange writing when you've met someone once. I can picture you—I have an idea of you in my head—I can hear how you sound and I have a sort of extension of this in the letter you've written.

I'm just in the middle of finishing a two-year relationship. We've kind of grown apart slowly and realized it as it happened—it's so civilized that it's a bit surreal. I suppose it's better than shouting and screaming. I don't think I'm good at relationships. I'm too searching and unsettled. I'm really going to enjoy being single again. Do my own thing with responsibility only to myself. I sometimes think our society is so relationship-orientated—the family and children etc. are everything. It's one way but why should it be accepted as the only way? As I get older so many friends are marrying and having kids I feel like I'm growing younger! I've been to about fourteen weddings in the last three years. Silly, I never feel it's going to happen to me!

Michèle, I hope this doesn't read too much as a rant and doesn't seem too self-indulgent—it's a bit stream of consciousness—maybe you'll feel you know me a bit better—I hope you can read it!

I'd like to take up where we left off—maybe go out on a night when you don't have to work the next day—for a full and proper dance. Some day!

Write again.

Love
Marcus

Hello again, Marcus …

I received your letter quite quickly. It only took a week to get to the States.

I am hand-writing this because I am no longer with the company. Oct 4 was my last day and, aside from the bands I'm singing with, I am officially unemployed. It's rather exciting for me, though. I'm entering a new phase of my life where I can't possibly know what lies around the corner. But then, I've always enjoyed that kind of existence. Luckily I have the total support of my family. The only thing that worries them is that I have no medical insurance. It worries me, too!

I'm glad to hear there's still a chance you will call NY your home. Please keep me posted. And remember there's nothing tying you down to one place. You're living for Marcus and Marcus alone. Isn't that wonderful?

I'll be sending you my demo once it's finalized. I have two tunes on it already that my friend recorded for me in Indiana and I'm waiting for my next live gig when I'll put a song on it. I want whoever hears it to see that my voice is the same in the studio as it is in a live performance. I think that's important. Too many artists overmix and change their voices in the studio. I like my finished product to sound like ME.

I'm not seeking fame (although that would be nice). I just wanna make a living and I really think I can. I feel like I'm versatile enough to get steady work. That's really all I'm looking for.

I had a great time in Indiana. I saw my dozen or so

close friends I miss dreadfully. Autumn in the Midwest is fabulous. I stayed at my friend's house on a lake. The trees had just started changing colors (COLOURS) and the temperature had dropped to the 50s and 60s. I love that. It's all cornfields and meadows and lots of trees out there. So nice to get away from the city once in a while. I want to have easy access to a city for the rest of my life, but I'm just as much a country girl.

It's flattering that you write to me considering you claim that you don't write much. And don't worry—you don't sound over-indulgent. I like that you just go off with your thoughts and write as if you're speaking. It shows me you're real. It's giving me insight into who you are. I can only vaguely picture you. You wore black and had a hat on most of the night. You had a buzz-cut or something close to it, and your hair is either blonde or strawberry blonde. You're thin and you had tons of energy. But that's about as much as I recall of your physical traits. What I remember most is your person. I enjoyed you so much. You were like my pal right from the get-go. Such a pleasure …

Being single is a great thing. Some people can't do it—or are afraid to do it. Many people lose themselves in their relationships and forget who they are, instead of learning from the other person and bettering themselves. The last relationship I was in (the last REAL one) was really wonderful, but we were so young and heading really quickly toward marriage. Neither of us was ready at that stage of our lives. We got along great, total trust, devotion, honesty, fun, etc. everything a solid relationship needs. It was just at the wrong time. He just moved to LA. He's my very best friend, but I can tell we're growing apart. I tell myself that if something's meant to happen, it'll happen.

I have a lot of faith in fate. That doesn't mean we should just sit back and watch the world pass us by, but it does mean that we can't control everything.

Anyway, now that I've been single for a while I'm really enjoying it. I like being my own person, but I do have one significant worry. I fear that because I'm so picky—because I don't give out my number and flirt with drunks in bars—and I have insufferably high standards because I know what I want and I know what I DON'T want—I'm going to end up alone.

I know what a good relationship is, and it can be so beautiful, so fulfilling. I definitely want it again someday, but I fear I won't get it. I'm not the type to have one-night stands or date more than one guy at once. So if I start seeing someone I'm either gonna really like him and want things to progress, or I'm gonna not like him and want things to end right away. I'm just not into the grey area. It's either really RIGHT, or really NOT right. I want children someday, so badly that I would be a single parent if it came to that.

You know, you can be "searching and unsettled" with someone. Never forget that.

Well, now that you know everything about me (hardly, we haven't even scratched the surface, my friend), we should have plenty to discuss upon your arrival in NY (assuming that happens sometime soon).

Here's a tip: go for a run at about 4pm. I just returned from the Park (Central, that is) after a

2½-mile run amidst the sights and smells of autumn, my favorite time of year. Dead leaves under my feet, gold and red looming high above me, the sun sparkling through the cracks in the canopy of colors, ah it is truly glorious. It only lasts about three or four weeks here and then winter is upon us. The season of death and gloom.

Thank god for the Park. Otherwise this city would really irk me.

I returned to the apartment and, with a glass of water, sat down to write you because my head felt so clear and crisp and serene. I wish I was like this 24 hours a day.

Enough. I'll let you get on with your day. I hope all is well for you out there in Merry Old England. I do so hope to visit some day, but I have no $$ as of late, so it'll be a while. We'll have to wait 'til your return. I hope it's soon …

Stay happy and healthy and write soon.

Thank you for your sweet, thoughtful, wise words. I hope the distance between us doesn't deter our friendship from progressing …

Love,
Michèle

Dear Michèle,

Thanks for your wonderful letter. I sat and read it after a day's work, lying on the floor in my flat.

I hope you are surviving OK without working. You've made a brave decision. I think it is sometimes more difficult to give something up than to carry on in something you hate—especially when it is your living and financial stability—I hope you find something that deserves you.

You say you remember me having tons of energy. That's quite a compliment from you, as I recall you chatting at a taxi driver until he revealed his life history to you and sang your praises (clearly captivated by you) for the rest of the journey—such a clear but fading memory of a life-affirming week!

You talked about the country–city split in you. I was born and brought up in the south-west of England—a large wilderness full of heather and gorse and rocky hills stretching away as far as you can see. I spent my childhood outdoors and fairly undisturbed by city life. I go back there as my family still lives there. I feel my spiritual batteries recharging—the tension of the city seems silly and self-indulgent when faced by beauty and wilderness. It is an old cliché I know, but I always feel it, and yet I'm drawn to live in the city (indeed to your city, the biggest and most intense of cities). I think I like to feel I am near what is going on.

I try and picture you reading this—there is a sense that as I write I try and get nearer to you, connect in my mind with you—your letters have given me a wider picture—it would be exciting to meet you again—but also probably quite strange as the reality of you is probably now divorced from your words and my images—it doesn't matter—it is nice to write and enjoy this process.

Michèle, I'm going to send this now. I'd like to write more, and I'll probably start another one. I really enjoyed your letter. I like what we are doing and I hope we can keep it going and develop … where are we going??!

Stay positive and happy.

Love
Marcus
XX

New light

Óscar left his apartment carrying the weight of his diving gear and feeling apprehensive. Why had he said yes? He had told Anna he was a good diver. They had never dived together, but they had lived together, for less than a year, and that didn't work out. They'd not seen each other since—he tried to identify the time, but he was not one to dwell on the past, he liked to look forward, they had separated bitterly—Anna had moved out last May.

It was almost a year on, spring. The air was feeling warmer. Barcelona was looking upwards to embrace the sunshine. Shopkeepers were polishing windows with ragged cloths and dousing doorsteps with buckets of bleachy suds. Tourists were beginning to arrive in search of Gaudí. A holiday coach idled at La Pedrera, passengers peering up at the bony facade and balustrades of black iron in tangled strips. Óscar had always seen the ironwork as ribbons, but today he thought of seaweed.

Anna had called him because she needed an extra diver.

The sea would still carry winter's chill in its currents, and visibility would be poor, but Óscar didn't mind. He adored diving and gave it the best of his free time away from the office, away from the climate-controlled marketing of pharmaceuticals, even in the icy months of January and February. It was the closest he could feel to flying, the weightless floating breath of it. It was liberating. The Costa Brava was no tropical reef, but there was a good wreck and protected natural areas to explore. Óscar enjoyed the feeling of discovery as new worlds appeared suddenly over wavering cliffs.

He had wondered about Anna, almost missed her. But today was not about her. She needed help, that was all, and he could not refuse. Óscar would be the only diver who was not a medical practitioner. The others were physiotherapists and doctors. For all of them, diving was an easy sport they could take for granted. Today they would be guides for two physically disabled men.

Óscar drove out through Barcelona's eastern suburbs and headed north in the direction of Girona. It was good to escape the city. The sky was wide, clear-glazed, and every detail of the dark green mountains seemed sharp in the spring light: the stones of an abandoned finca crumbling into a slope, the splash of spilt white paint on a roadside sign, wildflowers.

When he took the turning east, he felt apprehensive again. Not about Anna. He had lived without her for almost a year. What was past was past. They had travelled to deserts together. *Why deserts?* he wondered now. He didn't know. He remembered a photo he'd taken of her in Namibia, standing with a local woman. They both frowned a little, and their bodies were angled in a perfect parallel.

Namibia, Botswana, Libya, Mongolia ... Óscar and Anna had loved the extremes of places without water on the planet's exposed surface. The opposite of diving. He had never dived with her before. The very fact of this now struck him as peculiar. Perhaps it was the cause of his apprehension.

Past the resort gearing up for summer, half empty, half awake—*camping, diving, sailing, cambio, cambio, change*—the bay opened up in bright Mediterranean blue. Anna was already at the club with the others. They were gathered outside in the car park. She looked the same as always, maybe a little thinner. Her hair was short and neatly cut. Her fine-boned face was pale against the black of her wetsuit. She introduced Óscar to the other volunteers, already in their wetsuits: Assumpció, Xavier and Caterina. She introduced him to the diving students: Bartomeu and Remei. It was odd to see Anna in a crowd like this—she wasn't very sociable and she didn't like groups. Óscar hadn't thought to ask her how long it was since she'd started the club.

"You're the freshman here today," she said to him, direct as ever. "Assumpció is a physio like me. The other two are doctors."

"But I make up for it with my bedside manner," Óscar laughed, still feeling uncertain.

Remei smiled supportively. He was wearing a bright red tracksuit and chunky white running shoes. He had a big nose and a big smile, laughter lines around his eyes, the look of a comedy actor. His face moved expressively but his whole body remained unnervingly still in the wheelchair.

"I'm in your team," he said to Óscar.

"Alongside me and Anna," said Caterina. "Nice to meet you."

"You drew the short straw," Remei said dryly. "Which is some kind of visual irony, given my height."

Remei was huge. He looked tall and he was carrying a lot of weight. He'd been permanently paralysed in a car accident years earlier. Óscar tried to imagine losing muscle power from his neck to his toes and fingertips. He'd never been so close to disability. He felt conscious of looking, seeing, staring, not staring.

"These guys have never been diving before," said Anna. "They're total beginners, so they're a bit nervous, but they've heard you're good."

"Oh, I'm good," said Óscar, shifting his weight from foot to foot on the cement.

"We're only nervous because we're trying to impress Anna," said Bartomeu. He spun his wheelchair around on the spot, a pirouette. "I'm showing off now because I know I'll be all over the place underwater." He had tattoos on his neck, a ripped sleeve shirt, long wavy hair and a thick beard.

Óscar thought of Neptune, the mighty rippling torso that shouldered the weight of marble fountains.

"Your main challenge will be to limit your strength," Anna said to Bartomeu. "In fact, you'll barely have to think about going up, or down, or sideways, and you will. You'll have to think small, very, very small."

"If you think insinuation," Óscar added, "you'll still get exaggeration."

"I should warn you I'm a bit claustrophobic," Remei

said. "There's something about depending on that little tube of air for my oxygen that makes me panic. And chewing on that mouthpiece. I tried it in the pool."

"Lots of people feel the same way, especially on the first dive," said Caterina.

Anna said: "If you find you can't get past that feeling, just say. You can pull out at any time."

"I wouldn't miss it for the world," said Remei. "Mind over matter."

"And it's worse for control freaks!" Anna smiled.

"I was the same," Óscar said. "Once you get past the surface, the worry should go. You'll feel free as a bird."

Remei and Bartomeu looked at each other, and their wheelchairs, and laughed.

"Assumpció and Xavier will accompany you, Bartomeu." Anna pointed as she spoke, which helped Óscar remember their names. Assumpció was fair, balding. Xavier was dark. He had a deep scar running through his eyebrow.

"I've done a lot of things in my time," Bartomeu said. "But I never thought I'd go diving."

"You'll be using your eyes for signals," Anna said. "We'll be doing the same, Remei."

Óscar admired her emotional efficiency, her directness. It got her into trouble sometimes, lost her friends, he knew that. He was much more careful about keeping people on his side, avoiding offence.

"Everything is different with scuba. It's an inverse universe." Anna glanced at the others. "I say this every dive, don't I?"

"Just for the last two years!" said Assumpció.

"Before my time," Xavier smiled.

Anna continued. "All the instincts you need as an animal to survive on land are problematic when you're pretending to be a fish."

Óscar watched as she explained the destructive power of land panic: fight-or-flight hormones, accelerated breathing, the rush to escape, any rash movement, even the desire to call or cry out—it was all dangerous at ten metres below sea level. She was beautiful to watch, calming, clear. He remembered the day she moved out of his flat. *I'll pack my things and go back to my parents*, she'd said. No door-slamming, no dramatic gestures. They'd been fighting for months, blaming each other for everything. He'd spent himself on work, came home late for it, lived months abroad for it, put it first. He'd accommodated her, allowed her some space in his territory. But it was a bachelor's flat. She'd never felt at home. He realized now that in their time living together he'd not taken any interest in her work as a physiotherapist. They'd not dived together. He hadn't even known about her volunteering. He wondered now how many other things he'd missed.

It took more than an hour to help Remei prepare for his dive. Óscar, Anna and Caterina lifted him out of his wheelchair and fitted him with a harness to stabilize his weight and prevent him from falling. Óscar was impressed at the strength and skill of the two trained women; he was their feeble assistant. They oiled Remei's skin to help ease on the wetsuit. Remei made jokes about being upright for a change, and the fine art of lubrication. He used to love motorbikes when he was young. His wife would be jealous.

Their boat was equipped with a hydraulic diving platform. Anna jumped first. She watched as Bartomeu's team followed, organized themselves, then began their slow descent.

"You ready to get wet, Remei?" Anna called up to the boat.

Remei nodded.

Óscar was feeling apprehensive. His wetsuit felt uncomfortable and the sea seemed to slap the boat, lightly, indecisive. Deep blue. Deep green. This way. Then that.

Óscar and Caterina attached themselves with nylon ropes to Remei's harness. When they jumped, Remei fell heavily into the water. Óscar imagined being Remei, for a moment glimpsing the man's physical vulnerability and superhuman trust. He looked across to Caterina and together they steadied Remei in the slap-slap of the water.

Óscar felt suddenly useful and light. "How are you doing?" he asked.

"Fine." Remei looked downward at his air supply. "Still not sure about these tubes, though. And these weights! Don't I weigh enough already?"

"Take your time," said Óscar. "There's no rush."

"And you just tell me the moment you want to get out," said Anna, treading water, close now.

Remei blinked the escape signal.

"Only joking," he said. "And before you say anything,

I promise not to make eyelid jokes down there. Now let's deal with this … pacifier."

Anna carefully fitted his mask and air supply. Remei dry-retched. She released the regulator. He took slow, calm breaths of sky air. They tried again. He gulped and coughed.

Óscar remembered his first dive. He had overcome his claustrophobic reflex by lowering his face and slipping in the mouthpiece at the water's surface just at the point of submersion.

"Let's try it like this," he said.

It was Anna's task to swim ahead of Remei, studying his eyes for specific movements signalling joy or discomfort, problems with air or pressure, time to quit. She was to share her air if he needed it, clear his mask when the glass steamed up, and help him equalize on the descent. Óscar and Caterina were to watch and respond to Anna's eyes and hand signals, keeping Remei balanced all the time.

The water was an intense blue. The light filled Óscar with wonder, pouring from above in unreal rays, criss-crossing their descent. He thought of holy cards, the divine illumination of clouds, beams streaming from a saint's open hands—an eel slipped past him. A school of tiny fish darted, rose and scattered like a shower of silver coins. But Óscar was not here to daydream or sightsee.

They made careful progress downwards, stopping regularly to equalize the pressure in their heads. They reached fifteen metres and paused.

Visibility was good. Óscar hadn't expected that. Ahead

he could see Bartomeu, advancing with his arms in crustacean motion, a tank on his broad back, hair streaming up and behind him, Assumpció and Xavier flanking him like exotic fish.

Óscar wanted to gasp, or clap, or laugh, or shout, but he knew he couldn't do any of those things.

He watched Anna's eyes as she watched Remei's eyes. She signalled with her hand to move and they settled into the dive. Óscar kept watching Anna's eyes watching Remei's eyes. She never lost focus. The bubbles rose past her face in even exhalations, timed with Remei's breaths, neat and beautiful as a couple waltzing. Anna's gestures guided Remei's gaze to the gleam of eels, a baby octopus, lobsters, starfish, a forest of black seaweed as restless as a Gaudí balcony. Óscar and Caterina settled into their own rhythm, following Anna's signals, making eye contact with each other, balancing and adjusting tension, working as one. Óscar felt like the limb of a single complicated organism, soaring in a sky.

Back on the boat, Remei said, "I did something I didn't think I'd ever do." The laughter lines bunched around his eyes. "I spend my days sitting in a chair and today I took off."

Caterina nodded. "You're a natural."

Bartomeu squeezed the water from his hair. "I felt so light, I moved in three dimensions! Amazing."

"This has to be one of the best days of my life," said Remei.

"Me too," said Óscar. He could gasp or clap or laugh or shout now, without causing danger for anyone, but he felt quiet, intensely happy.

"Thanks," Remei said. "It was tough at the start, but I got to see things I thought I'd never see."

"Me too," said Óscar, "thanks to you."

He looked at Anna as she relaxed. She was pleased with the dive. There had been no troubles, no setbacks.

She looked back at him. Her expression was pensive, contented, almost surprised. "It's good having an extra diver around," she said. "Would you join us again?"

Two interiors

~ ❦ ~

This is the tale of two women in love.

They are both professors.

The romance starts in 1987. Spring, the season of tulips.

The characters refer to themselves in passing as Zig and Zag—a transposed verbal relic from ancient Australian television—but these two women are nothing like the TV clowns who flogged ice cream to a nation of little children, even if they do like to laugh and cry more openly than most. They might as well be Tip and Top, or Chalk and Cheese. They look nothing like each other.

Rosi is a nomadic Italian. She is dark, curvaceous, carnivorous, Catholic.

Back in 1960-something, fresh off the boat from Italy, the transported girl must have felt foreign as she watched Zig and Zag, with their studio audience of Australian children chanting jingles in English. It was not remotely stylish to be foreign then. For Rosi, Australianness meant dislocation and distance. From a suburban high school to the National University in Canberra, she scholarshipped her way back to Europe, studied and taught at the Sorbonne, enjoyed a swinging swinging-single life in Paris, published philosophical texts in three languages and finally added Dutch to her repertoire.

Anneke is a Dutchwoman with 'clogs in the clay'—she's a homebody, she stays put. She is blonde, tall, slim, vegetarian, Protestant (now Buddhist).

She grew up expecting to be a wife and a bearer of children. Her father was a professor and her mother his loving support. Anneke went to college and learned to administrate; she learned intellectual ambition later. She was a confirmed hippy, openly bisexual, embracing the freedoms that came in the years after the sexual revolution and before AIDS.

In Holland, there is a tradition: people have no screens on their front windows. No closed shutters, no curtains, no blinds. At most there is a gauzy layer that can be seen through. The friend on the street, the neighbour, the postman and the tourist can all equally look into the interior life of others because (apparently) there is nothing to hide.

Rosi and Anneke both see through the see-through. They are philosophers. It's their job to do so. They are doubtful of the moral gloss. They suspect it of faint hypocrisy and snobbery, a kind of parlour purity that reflects the traditional Protestant notion of grace and favour.

Anneke and Rosi steam up the glass, they let it clear, they reveal their agonies and ecstasies, their contradictions and their two interiors. They laugh.

ANNEKE: "The first time I saw Rosi, I was still a student at Utrecht. She was giving a lecture in a church, a classic Dutch church, white, empty and very cold. It was the most brilliant

lecture I'd ever heard. My heart was beating fast. She was very funny. She was wearing this horrific purple woollen scarf and a very old, very ugly, brown leather coat—"
ROSI: "No it was black! It was a black coat, and woollen, not leather. I've still got the brown leather one in the archive. It was the first purchase I'd ever made with my own money. I bought it at Myers department store, in Melbourne, when I was a student."
ANNEKE: "Anyway, here was a woman who kept her coat on all the way through her lecture."
ROSI: "It was cold!"
ANNEKE: "The impression was that this was someone who was about to walk out at any moment."
ROSI: "Anyway I didn't care about clothes then."
ANNEKE: "I became a teacher at the university. The Chair became available and I heard that Rosi had applied for it. I was so excited to have someone like that in the department. At the end of the interviewing procedures there were two candidates left. They were both asked to give one more lecture."
ROSI: "This older woman philosopher fought me to the end. It was quite protracted, tortuous."
ANNEKE: "Rosi's lecture was amazing. The committee asked our opinion and we all chose Rosi. There were all these people in the corridor and in the middle of chatting I suddenly heard this voice. I remember how grey the building was, how bureaucratic-feeling, for such an extraordinary emotional experience. There was this voice outside my head, distinct but not loud, surrounded by silence, and the voice said: *This is the woman who will take you away from H—.* I was overwhelmed. H— was my boyfriend, we were living

together, we'd bought a house and I was trying to get pregnant and start a family. We were moving away from hippiedom towards a more bourgeois existence."

ROSI: "I came in from Paris. I was considering this move to the most unlikely of places—Holland!"

ANNEKE: "The staff were invited to lunch with all these professors. I was at the same table as Rosi. She had already lived in Italy, Australia and Paris, and now she was prepared to come to Holland—I wondered what kind of person she must be. She could just keep packing up and moving. Did she have no friends? But she had a friendly face. I was looking at her and thinking this when suddenly she looked at me and winked. I blushed."

ROSI: "You heard voices—but I saw light, this amazing light effect. I saw you surrounded by light, wearing flaming yellow clothes, a bright yellow top that shone like an angel, so blindingly light I practically had to wear sunglasses—"

ANNEKE: "I don't even have a yellow top."

ROSI: "Maybe I was winking at you because the light was so bright!"

ANNEKE: "I look awful in yellow."

ROSI: "I needed sunglasses! I felt this wonderful sense of connection, light, warmth, clever friendliness. Of course it wasn't until much later that I sent you a postcard from Paris."

ANNEKE: "I laughed with my boyfriend. I said, *Ha! Rosi's flirting with me!*"

ROSI: "I was in my seventh year of psychoanalysis. I started the new job part-time, commuting, one week Paris, one week Utrecht, so the analysis halved. It's the classic resolution of a psychoanalytic relationship—you bond, you begin a relationship with someone. My analyst said to me: *Prenez la vague! Catch the wave!* That's a nice surfing metaphor!"

ANNEKE: "So you came and you set up this department of women's studies."

ROSI: "I was the professor and there were two teachers, including Anneke. Just the three of us working very closely together. No place for a relationship."

ANNEKE: "You were always late. Everyone thought it was connected with being Italian."

ROSI: "It was always hit and run, always bumping into each other. It was becoming painful. One day I saw you wet in the rain. You were wearing a black leather jacket, very Amsterdam, very sexy. You were on your bicycle. Your hair was completely stuck to your head. You were shivering like a rabbit. I thought: *She needs me!* I wanted to save you."

ANNEKE: "We both wanted to save each other, because I vowed to save you from cynicism. I had this idea that you were about to turn bitter. I also made another vow: *I'm going to dress this woman!*"

ROSI: "I was overwhelmed by the job. I'd put on weight. Everything was one size too small so I looked like a mortadella."

ANNEKE: "You were on TV, performing all the time, lectures, it mattered. Your hair was flat."

ROSI: "I was working so hard, putting in sixty to seventy hours a week. I felt I had to honour the job. For ten years there wasn't time or space for much else."

ANNEKE: "I remember going down the stairs one day and thinking *I am falling in love.* You opened the door and almost jumped on me. We had a drink in the cafeteria—an old-fashioned bad deep-fried Dutch restaurant. We were talking and it suddenly got very intense—"

ROSI: "I had a gut feeling that you were going to be very important in my life. We went down to the basement and into the bicycle shed, this huge Dutch space full of bicycles. That's where we had our first kiss, in the bicycle shed!"

ANNEKE: "A sexual French kiss. I flew home. I was two hours later than normal. My boyfriend was pale. He was about to call the police, he was so worried. These were the days before mobile phones. I looked at him, thinking: *This is what I will do from now; I will hurt you.*"

ROSI: "It was an earthquake for me. City. Profession. Promotion. Relationship. I was thirty-three, a 'dangerous' postmodernist from Paris transposed to Holland to invent a programme. And I start by having a violently erotic affair with a subordinate. Nothing short of catastrophe."

ANNEKE: "It was a secret, except for my boyfriend. I didn't want to cheat on him. It had to be a secret at work. I didn't tell my family for a year, or my friends. My parents were relieved that I had turned out to be 'normal' at last. I wasn't prepared to leave my boyfriend. I was still trying to get pregnant. I tried for two years to balance both relationships. I still had this image of this woman with her coat on, like she was about to walk out at any moment."

ROSI: "And I was worried about my job. The amalgamation of relationship with job. Putting all my eggs in one basket. But meanwhile there was this overwhelmingly passionate sex. A lot of energy in the Utrecht programme came from the relationship. And many relationships sprang up later. This is one of the reasons for the success of the department. Such incredible passion you cannot formulate in a policy paper!"

ANNEKE: "And we are two very intense people."

ROSI: "I remember our first outing in Holland. It was still a secret relationship."

ANNEKE: "I borrowed my mother's car."

ROSI: "A flaming red little Skoda."

ANNEKE: "It was March. We went to the Kröller-Müller museum of modern art. Nothing was open so we ended up at a really tacky hotel."

ROSI: "The museum is in the middle of a park of fake bronze trees. It's surreal. There was nobody around, the car park was empty. It was cold. We had real sex in the car. It got so hot everything fogged up. All the windows were white. We were invisible."

ANNEKE: "But when we eventually emerged, the whole car park was full. We'd been oblivious to the outside world. People must have heard or noticed something. In the museum my knees collapsed—from too much sex! I mean so much sex you can't walk."

ROSI: "It was like that with us for a long time. We often joked *thank god we are over thirty*. If you were sixteen, you couldn't *hold* that sort of passion."

ANNEKE: "The sex was so passionate it bordered on violence. It was not vanilla. It was passion as suffering. The Passion."

ROSI: "I really often had to howl and cry."

ANNEKE: "I didn't know there was such depth to my emotions. You literally and emotionally entered me."

ROSI: "And you entered me. There was no way you could even have a membrane between us. No skin. No wall."

ANNEKE: "It was scary. It took us years to work it out."
ROSI: "Either you had to leave your job or I had to. And you had to leave your boyfriend."
ANNEKE: "He let me go, with pain in his heart. I went to live with my parents for three or four months."
ROSI: "Oh your mother was so cute!"
ANNEKE: "She said: *So you're going to live with your professor; you're a lesbian and there'll be no grandchildren.* Just like that. Actually, my parents came to accept it quite easily in the end."
ROSI: "You lived on your own for three years. We were both in our own separate space and yet in a relationship. In the beginning we could not have lived together. It was impossible."
ANNEKE: "It was too intense."
ROSI: "We would have torn each other apart."
ANNEKE: "And I had this huge fear. I had lost a relationship. I am accountable for hurting the man that I loved. I felt dearly for him. And I was scared of losing my job. I got a scholarship to write my PhD. And then I was unemployed. I had this fear that Rosi would move on and go elsewhere. I'd gambled everything. You know Jeanette Winterson's book *The Passion*? The gamble? We *played.* It took enormous courage to face all those risks and insecurities. It was only a few years later that I got a professorship."
ROSI: "Everything was in one bundle. I had to make a success of everything. If the relationship failed, then that would ruin the job. If the job failed, then that would ruin the relationship."
ANNEKE: "We decided to move in together in 1994. We'd calmed down. The passion was more manageable. Rosi

travelled so much we needed to live together in order to see each other at all. But we had to have separate quarters."
ROSI: "We found the magic house. Two kitchens, two bathrooms, two everything. We spent eight months looking. We bought it in twenty minutes."
ANNEKE: "When we started living together we started actually building the relationship."
ROSI: "Travel. Parties. Dinners. Social life. Family. Domesticated ..."
ANNEKE: "You can't *live* that wild passion."
ROSI: "It still flares up for days at a time. We want to kill each other. Then we have great sex and cry a lot."
ANNEKE: "I become murderous. My ego is threatened. I have no defences."
ROSI: "You perceive me as overwhelming."
ANNEKE: "My defence mechanism is raw anger, aggression, if it's negative. If it's positive, it's sexual."
ROSI: "We could just breathe."
ANNEKE: "We invented rituals to give the passion form and space."
ROSI: "Burning incense. Honouring what we have. Ritualizing everyday existence."
ANNEKE: "Flowers."
ROSI: "Candles."
ANNEKE: "Altars."
ROSI: "Gifts and poems that were nothing, to act out the pain, the intense love."
ANNEKE: "And gradually, literally, you build a home."
ROSI: "Art. Art is very important. And every Saturday I buy you a bunch of flowers. I go to the flower market, I buy you tulips, roses, freesias, it's very Dutch."

ANNEKE: "We had an engagement party after five years."
ROSI: "Gay marriage, excluding adoption, became possible in Holland in 1998. And we got married in 1999, the last year of the last century, the last year of the century of women—because the women's revolution was the only one that worked and the only one that had no victims. Our wedding date was 8th March, International Women's Day."
ANNEKE: "We felt strongly about the symbolism of it. There's something about the public ritual, that you've chosen each other, for life. We had a small ceremony with some family and friends as witnesses, a catered dinner at home—"
ROSI: "You said your Dutch family doesn't drink. Ha!"
ANNEKE: "We had cake and champagne. A classic three-tiered white wedding cake with marzipan, sponge and cream. And two statuettes of women on the top, both in white dresses and holding hands. The patissier had to order them specially."
ROSI: "Now there's an entire industry based on this. Double female statuettes. And double male. You can even get gay kissing couples in traditional Delft blue and white porcelain."
ANNEKE: "My father videotaped the wedding."
ROSI: "We made an edited video of the whole ceremony and party so that my parents could participate virtually from Melbourne. And your mother gave the speech welcoming me into the family. In Italian! She'd learned Italian specially to make the speech for my parents."
ANNEKE: "Well, not just for the speech, she was kind of learning Italian anyway."
ROSI: "In 2001, the process of gay marriage became

complete with the possibility of adopting, so the media called it 'real' gay marriage, which confused everyone. So we transferred our marriage over as a gesture. It matters. The difference is partly about the gaze of others. Better, because people's criticisms and anxieties are settled; worse, because some gays disapprove, and some straights say *it's OK for you but not for us …*"

ANNEKE: "I love you, I am your wife. But we do not adopt traditional husband and wife roles."

ROSI: "*More female than feminine*, as Virginia Woolf said of Vita."

ANNEKE: "Being married we act more as a couple, including when Rosi was knighted. And in the international *Who's Who* it says 'married to'."

ROSI: "We enjoy confronting the system with it because we are in high-profile positions."

ANNEKE: "We act formally as professors in our gowns. And at the Royal Gala with the Crown Prince and Princess we were there as a married lesbian couple."

ROSI: "We're very much a couple for so many people. We're a point of stability. A bit of an institution."

ANNEKE: "And yet the relationship means always changing together, working in the same direction."

ROSI: "It's work in progress. A philosophy of perpetual change. This taps into your Buddhism, and my restlessness."

ANNEKE: "The relationship is now nineteen or twenty years old. It shifts in time."

ROSI: "And without saying anything to each other, we suddenly started finding our house too big! We're ready to scale down, sell the magic house, get a small apartment."

ANNEKE: "At last we are ready to *really* live together—"

Rosi: "We are capable of being in the same space. One living room, one kitchen, one bathroom—"
Anneke: "Maybe two kitchens—"
Rosi: "Actually two bathrooms—well, definitely two toilets—and of course we need two studies—"

Political allies

~ ❦ ~

Zainab fell out with her boyfriend Hassan during the Iran–Iraq war. The relationship was on the rocks. Like her, he was an Iraqi, a writer and an activist, but she and he had different views. The reverberations travelled from the great and public and distant events, to the small and personal and local. There were divisions amongst all their friends. Some were glad of any opposition to President Saddam, anything at all to get rid of him. Some were happy to have a ceasefire. Others were worried about Iran taking over.

Reluctantly, Zainab went to a political meeting. She was not shy of politics, not at all, in fact she didn't know how to be politically inactive, but she wasn't too keen on the people who had organized this particular meeting. Most Iraqi exiles had been targeted in some way by one group or other, so she didn't know, she couldn't know, anyone's agenda.

The meeting house was in the London suburbs. It was decorated expensively in cream and gold, big and cold furnishings, Gulf style. Not Zainab's cup of tea at all. Everyone sat in a circle in the sitting room. There were women there, she observed. There were always women at these meetings. It satisfied some unspoken code of political correctness, but their views were always brushed aside. The business of war was always conducted by men.

"I am against both regimes," Zainab said to the group. "Because they are killing the people." She was never one for the ease of appeasement or political promotion. She had been imprisoned for being a dissident at just twenty years old.

People listened. One man in particular seemed to be sympathetic to her view. He was almost European in his manner.

"Who is he?" Zainab whispered to a friend sitting next to her.

"That's Mun'am," her friend whispered back.

"What's his story?"

"He teaches teachers. Maths. Head of Department. We call him the Englishman—he left Iraq in the 1960s."

Zainab slotted his emigration into the timeline: after the many coups that followed the revolution, long before her own escape to Syria and then England. How she and her comrades had envied the early exiles for having fun in free Europe!

Mun'am looked nice. His face was relaxed. Most Iraqis frowned when they talked. He wasn't frowning. He was pleasant to look at. He had a good smile that seemed to lighten him. He was sitting next to a religious man, a well-known cleric in full costume, who was very serious indeed. Mun'am did well by the contrast. Someone asked him about his health, not in a general greeting way, but in a particular way as if there were something significant to relate, something of concern. And people were asking bigger questions: what to do about the war? How to create change? Should they form a party? To what end?

Zainab would acknowledge that Saddam's government worked without the usual corruptions. He'd established campaigns to erase illiteracy, the best free health service in the area, an internationalist university funded by the oil boom—but all that came as one package with political oppression. Communist leaders, Marsh Arabs, rebellious Kurds in the north and Shias in the south had been suppressed, displaced, executed. Criminals had better treatment than dissidents, and the men who'd tortured and executed Zainab's comrades on behalf of the government had later been tortured and executed by the same government. She knew the liquid way of power. It ran in tricks like water, precious and capricious.

But that was no excuse for political inertia. She was Iraqi, Kurdish, intellectual, capable. She was a Marxist, a believer in Guevarism, not the Soviet style of Communism so beloved of dictators. As long as she could write and think and act, she would dream and hope. She would resist.

She went on a demonstration march near Hyde Park, a peaceful protest against the chemical bombardment of Halabja: five thousand Kurds, mostly women and children, had been killed, thousands of others maimed. More than one hundred thousand had fled to Turkey. Zainab was haunted by the images of poison attacking their skin, their eyes, their breathing, their nerves, their blood. It was the eighth year of the war. Nobody seemed to be taking any action against the abuses that had become daily business in Iraq.

Zainab saw Mun'am by chance in the crowd. He came up to her and shook her hand. They exchanged a few brief words and she knew he was an ally, driven by his hatred of oppression, and his love of Iraq. He distrusted professional politicians.

"Somehow when you see a politician kiss a baby, shake a hand—kiss *anything*—it is tainted," Mun'am said with a wry smile.

"I know exactly what you mean," Zainab said.

"Three thousand years ago, before Islam, we never bowed or kneeled to God. We stood directly with God as an equal and addressed the sky in an angry voice."

Better to die on your feet than live on your knees, Zainab thought. "It's the same now," she said, surveying the throng of exiled Iraqis still refusing to kneel.

"We are strong individual characters." Mun'am spoke lightly, gently, without a frown. "It's very difficult to force things on us. We have more than a drop of anarchism in our blood." He smiled again.

Zainab remembered a comrade who was tortured and executed when he was twenty-four, a friend whose fair face and generous laughter she knew she could never forget. When she'd met him for the first time, half her life ago, in the silence of Iraqi midday heat, she had thought: *At last, a comrade who can laugh and not feel guilty about it!*

Zainab was always remembering things. Beautiful things like perfumed gardens with vines and pomegranates, the labyrinth of alleys in the city, the mirror-springs and coloured mountains of Zino where children sold snow in the summer, the fish and fern-filled clear streams of Nawchilican. And Zainab remembered terrible things, such terrible things that for years she did not sleep at night without pills. And then she dreamed, dark dreams, faces and sounds and sensations that would not let her go.

Her miserable boyfriend had become exasperated, berated her for living in the past. Hassan was right. The present was ghostly for her, insubstantial, immaterial. She inhabited the past with her body and her brain. It was more real.

Zainab had written out her memories. Her stories were surrealistic and journalistic by turns. She'd been in London for more than ten years. She wrote about travelling with her father when she was a child. She wrote about her time as a guard in the resistance, itching from bedbugs, bearing weapons, defending her right to be a woman and a soldier. She wrote about her time as a political prisoner in the prisons of Abu Ghraib and Qasr al-Nihaya, the Palace of the End, when human howls sounded through her days and nights, and friends were brought before her, one by one, damaged by torture, as she was. She wrote about her fearful mother, who sat with a box of clothes and food for her outside the prison walls, all day, every day, sweating in the heat, knowing that the neighbours shunned her for fear of guilty association, but persisting until the guards admitted that her daughter was inside, alive. Zainab wrote about her time in prison with women caged en masse, like animals, nowhere to lie down or sleep. They protected her, gave her a corner where she could lean and rest, told her about the abusive men they'd killed in passion or self-defence, the extra sentence of vengeance that awaited them after jail. Zainab wrote about her release: her blindfolded journey towards her presumed execution, her escape to Syria, her flight to

London, the damp soggy mossiness of London, the double-decker buses, the safe but long and sleepless nights.

Some time after the Halabja peace demo, Zainab had friends to stay, Iraqi exiles from Germany. They slept on the floor of her tiny London flat, all six of them, filling up the space with bedding and baggage. They agreed that other Iraqis and Arabs were conspicuous in their silence about what was happening to the Kurds. Why were they so inert? Together they came up with an idea for a book—a collaborative publication of condemnation, a chorus of voices, artists and writers and thinkers.

"You should ask Mun'am to contribute," Jassim the poet suggested.

Zainab had seen Mun'am twice, so she knew who he was, but she didn't have his number.

"I'll call him," said Jassim.

Mun'am was in the throes of divorce and had just moved into a new flat. He invited them all over for dinner.

When they got there, Zainab was surprised to see that there was no dinner at all. Instead, the table was heaped with raw ingredients, piles of spring onions, bunches of parsley, basil, mint, all the colourful things in the middle. Everyone chopped and cooked together. It reminded her of making sandwiches as kids. The mood was almost festive.

"What a great atmosphere!" Mun'am kept saying. "This is like when we were students!"

They had all been members of the same opposition group in Baghdad. They discussed life and friends and different countries and politics. It felt good. Zainab relished the discourse—it was intellectual and interesting. They wrote poetry together and made a video, stayed up late, until at last she took her house guests back home.

The next day Mun'am phoned at seven o'clock, nice and early. Zainab's poor visitors were sleeping by the telephone.

"What are you planning to do today, all of you?" Mun'am asked. He was far too awake. He organized outings to do as a group, Zainab included.

He did the same thing every day for six days: first the early-bird call, then the group activities.

You don't do that just for political activism, Zainab thought. *He must be lonely.*

One night, they sat around the table, after yet one more hearty meal. They were talking about travelling. Zainab had never thought about travelling for the sake of it, but she needed a holiday.

"I want to go to Andalucía," she said.

Hassan didn't want to go anywhere.

For the first time Zainab realized she didn't really care how miserable he was.

"Anyone else interested?" She threw the question to the group. It felt frivolous, impulsive. She imagined them all straggling off together, noisy and chatty.

But the group was quiet.

"I've always wanted to go to Spain," Mun'am said. "But I don't want to do it on my own. I'm nearly fifty and I've just got my British passport—at last!"

They set off as friends.

They talked all the way to Spain. They discovered that they had similar tastes in food and music. They were political twins. They valued the culture of scepticism and doubt. They believed in the force of the mind, not the promotion of faith. They'd both gone to the same little school years ago, a delicious coincidence, although Mun'am had been there eight years ahead of her. It was in the middle of the district that became the heart of resistance in Baghdad. They felt at home with each other. They laughed and joked. They were on a coach when Mun'am leaned his head on Zainab's shoulder. The moment felt warm and natural. They arrived in Seville without any accommodation booked. The place was packed with visitors for the *feria*. Eventually the two friends found a bed.

They came back to London as lovers.

I'd like to know more about Zainab and Mun'am in Seville and Grenada, the expression of passion that disrupted their politics, but sprang from it. I can picture them finding joy in a shabby *hostal* with no stars, dancing at the *feria*. Or wandering dreamily through the green and fragrant courtyards of the Alhambra, with the incessant sound of fountains, water trickling, splashing, playing.

But they are private people and their passion is a secret.

"I'm useless in romance." Mun'am sips a little coffee, looks affectionately at Zainab. They have been living together for sixteen years. He is retired now. They are still very much in love.

Their London home is an oasis: a plain house in a terrace surrounded by urban motorways and hyperstores. Their living room is draped with rugs. Light pours in from skylights and windows, added as birthday presents, from him to her.

"I don't know how to woo a woman. It happens without me knowing. I remember the first time being aware of something. She leaned her head on my shoulder, or I leaned on her, I'm not sure which. It was our first physical contact. I must have fallen for her without noticing. I felt warmth and oddness. I was aware of feeling tenderness and aware of being aware, judging myself and thinking: *Is this right?* Wondering whether this was going to spoil a friendship or whether I could be any good with a relationship. I'd been lonely, gradually cutting my links with most of the Iraqis. I had become withdrawn, bottled up, dry. All my dreams had the theme of dryness. I knew she had a relationship with Hassan, not a solid one, but I felt I might be encroaching. And yet it felt natural to be with her like this. We talked and talked and talked. She listened! I felt at home."

"He was looking for Iraqiness," Zainab says. "Most men fall in love with their mothers."

She's delighted to talk about her love for Mun'am—it's a happier subject than Iraq. She has just returned from the United Nations Human Rights Council, where she gave a paper about the effects of war and occupation on women, the impact on health and education.

"I was what he missed. He was what I missed. We felt totally at home with each other. He'd been to a homeopath who said he couldn't help him because he was too cerebral. Isn't that interesting? I think it was because he couldn't deal with the Iran–Iraq war that he had a brain haemorrhage in 1988. That's why, back at the political meeting, when we met for the first time, people were asking him about his health. When we went on holiday I thought: *he's gorgeous*. I didn't have to prove myself or pretend. We were so open. I was laughing all the time at his Englishness, his willingness to talk openly about everything. In our culture, socially we go round and round, we never say things straight. When he gets excited with a new idea, he is full of life and no one can catch up with him. He's very dynamic. I'm a slow person. We complement each other. It's so healthy. We have fresh ideas. Fear grows like a weed and it's easy to despair at what's happening in Iraq today, but we both have hope. We both dream of a better world."

PE

New York, London III

~ ⚘ ~

Hi, Marcus.

Wow. Your letter came at a time when I probably needed it most. My life is so weird right now. Very transitional. I started this waitressing job and although it's a high-priced restaurant and I like 90% of the people I work with, I'm not getting the hours I want, nor the money I expected. So I'm doing my best to sub for people and pick up as many shifts as I can. The managers have unfortunately pigeonholed me into cocktail waitressing and won't put me in the dining room. I'm totally broke ($80 in the bank and $30 in my wallet). I haven't been able to do a mass mailing of my headshots to agents in the city because of this, and that's bad because it's the only way I'm going to be able to attend really good auditions. I feel a bit lost. Luckily I have a supportive family and when push comes to shove they help me out. But that's a LAST resort. I don't like asking for money and I certainly don't like owing it.

I've been feeling lonely lately, and although the opportunity to date comes my way frequently (sorry if *that sounds like I'm boasting, I'm NOT, believe me, anyone can get asked out by a bunch of losers) it isn't flattering and leaves me unexcited about the prospects of finding a real companion. I don't mean a husband (I'm only 24!), I mean someone to <u>hang</u> with.*

So your letter gave me a little ego boost, a smile, a resurgence of fond memories, and the notion that perhaps my pickiness concerning male companionship is a good thing after all.

What is happening here, Mr London?

You are such a great writer. I write to you with your letter in front of me. I feel almost incompetent, like I can't nearly express myself as you can. I love what you say about your spiritual batteries recharging. That's perfect. Perfect.

Where do you read my letters? Do you get your mail on your way out or on your way in? I'm curious. I put all aside, get out my specs and just sit 'til I've finished every word. In fact, I read your letters several times so as to get the flow of the whole thing, to get your tone, and to benefit from your beautiful, fitting choice of words and phrases. Such eloquence.

It's unclear to me just how different your work in NY would be than what you do right now in England. I'd love a description if you can find the time to jot it down.

Meeting you again would no doubt be strange. Lots of high expectations, I suppose. Fear of disappointment. But there's gotta be some strong reason as to why you and I connected as we did that night. Perhaps the force still exists and would allow us to re-connect upon our next meeting. Let's hope so.

It's now after 1am and I'm home, picking up right where I left off. Work was very hectic. I ran non-stop for the entire evening.

If you come to NY permanently (or semi-permanently) I promise to show you calmer places so you can get out of this crazy place once in a while and catch your breath! I don't know how much you've seen of this country—or this part of the country, meaning the east coast—but there's just so much.

Well, my handwriting is getting worse, so I guess that means I'm tired. I'll be going to a movie tomorrow with my 15-year-old stepsister before I'm off to face grandma so I should probably get some sleep. I've so enjoyed writing you. I always do. I feel as though I'm actually speaking to you. I like you, Marcus. At least, I like how you're presenting yourself to me. Let's see if you're a big phoney! Just kidding.

Smile.

Lots of love,
Michèle

Dear Michèle

I read your letter last night after I got back from a weekend in Cornwall. I threw my stuff on the floor, fell onto my bed and read it all the way through. It gave me a big smile and a spring in my step! I was really pleased that I helped cheer you up a bit—I hope by now that is not necessary and you feel better—I suppose the "transitional stage" lasts longer than a few weeks and I'm sure you will still be feeling uneasy—as you say to me, I hope you feel totally comfortable about writing with how you are feeling—I think it can help formulate plans and evaluate your situation besides keeping me happy!!

I've read your letter a few times now—I tend to read very fast first of all—sort of greedily and excitedly—than after the feel from that I go back and read again and feel it more—the second reading brings the smile and buzz!

What auditions have you got coming up? What are they like? Are they like a row of people watching you walk onto a stage from the auditorium as you announce yourself and tell them what you're going to sing? Have I been watching too many 1950s films? I can imagine you holding yourself well—you come across as confident and self-assured—I remember you walking down the street outside the club after you'd gone to find a cash machine—you ambled along looking lost in your thoughts and totally at one with yourself and what you were doing—if you could get that across to anyone I'm sure you'll be right there! I'd like to see your 'headshots'—do they capture this? Do they capture you?

I like your idea of a relationship as "someone to hang with". It's a difficult balance though—the person you love to be with, who entertains you and makes you laugh, but you really cannot fancy, however hard you try—or the person with whom you have so much passion and sexual energy and yet you're bored stupid with them at other times—is it possible to have both the positives? I still don't know and I'm what, six years older than you?! I think some people become satisfied with a compromise—have you seen 'Husbands and Wives'? Carry on being picky my dear—it's the way to be—don't make excuses for the parts of someone you don't like. "I'll change them." "They'll come right." It doesn't happen. It just festers.

I hope we can find some time to "just hang" soon (such an American expression—I love it!) I wonder how we'd relate. Would we chat coyly like strangers unsure where we are—or talk away freely and openly with connecting glances—who knows? I hope it will be wonderful!

Sorry, I wrote "my dear" up above—it just came out—I sound like an old queen!

What do I do? I'm a lawyer specializing in representing children charged with criminal offences (aged 10–17). I attend at the police station when they are arrested and advise them what to do/say when questioned—then represent them in court—make bail applications, do trials and sentencing hearings. I do some work with adults when I have to, but I try and avoid it. At least when you deal with kids there is the possibility of change and of being some part in assisting that change. I do take my work very seriously—I enjoy it a lot but it is very emotionally draining. I find it gives me a warped perspective on life sometimes.

It's late now—I'm still at my table and I'm going to move to my bed. I love my flat—it's costing me at the moment as it's having building work, but it's my space and my place. I can do my thing here—walk around as I want, talk to myself, sing and make big dance tunes! I've got two bedrooms—one of which is my recording studio. How is your place? Do you share it or is it your own place?

So Michèle—when shall we meet again? I like the idea of you showing me your country—it is a nice fantasy at the moment and warms me. I like what's happening here—this night's meeting, this exploration of each other through written words—how different this is from face-to-face exploration—isn't it possible to present as a phoney just as easily in person? I think it is more difficult to be phoney in writing—I'm not doing it!! I'm just opening up on paper—if you stop writing then I'll know you don't like it—you'll always be free to do that!! If you carry on writing letters like your last one though it's going to get frustrating—I want to see this girl again!!

What is happening, Ms Manhattan?

Anyway, I hope to hear from you soon—I look forward to it. If you feel lonely or pissed off then write—even call?—I'll call you back—I don't know, maybe we shouldn't speak!?!

Whatever, I'll be thinking of you.

Love
Marcus
xx

My gosh, Marcus ...

Your last letter arrived so quickly. Much faster than I'd expected it to. Thank you so much.

I just finished paying several bills and going over my finances for the next month (oh, joy and rapture!). Much to my chagrin, I don't see how I'm going to cover everything. It's quite frightening, really. Every month I have a slight panic attack like this and yet every month things seem to get paid, so perhaps I'm worrying unnecessarily.

I actually received your letter a week ago and have just now found the time to respond. I've been working like a dog! My hours are crazy and although I love the restaurant and all my co-workers, it doesn't seem to be paying off for me monetarily.

Meanwhile, there have been family obligations with which I've had to deal in the past few weeks. My maternal grandmother was admitted to the geriatric psych ward at Mt Sinai hospital here in NY. That's had a bad effect on my mother. Thanksgiving came and went and, since my parents are divorced, I had to clear up two days instead of one so I could attend both sides' gatherings. My oldest sister asked me to dog-sit for five days, but I could barely keep him under any kind of control. So I'm over-worked, underpaid, and very, very tired. I've gained 5lbs from the holiday and from not having the time to fit a run in. I feel like a slug. Enough whining ...

In answer to your questions, yes, the auditions are generally as you're picturing them. The number of people varies from audition to audition. Most of the time I feel confident. I hope I exude that! A few days ago I was waiting on a 3-top and the man at the table said to me: "You look like an actress." And thinking he was saying I look like an existing actress, I asked, "Who?" And he said "No, I mean you yourself look like an actress." I said: "Thanks so much. Are you a casting director?" And he said no. And I said: "Then what the hell am I talking to you for?" We had a good laugh, and it was a compliment nonetheless.

My apartment is a large (for NYC, that is) one-bedroom that has been changed to two. My roommate's brother made the dining room into a bedroom by putting a wall up (a thin wall, unfortunately). I'll admit I'd love my own place, but I can't afford it and probably won't for a long time. Even a small studio in NY will run you a bundle.

I wonder how our meeting up will be. That's why I'm afraid to speak with you by phone. I do believe you're someone I want to continue to know, so keep writing as you do and if we meet again and are disappointed, well, at least we've had these wonderful letters and have benefited from them. No regrets! Sometimes I try to picture your voice—hear you saying the words you've written in your British accent—and I can't get a clear sound. How could I possibly remember your voice after only a few hours together?

I had this dream the other night that I went to England and saw you. But you weren't you. I mean, you looked completely different. I was staying with a married couple who were disgusted with the fact that I was in their house with my shoes off (I never wear shoes in my own house, I love being barefoot). I was unaware that in England it's considered gauche to be barefoot indoors. It's not, is it?

I'm contemplating sending you my headshots. Part of me wants you to have a clear picture of what I look like, but part of me wants to keep you guessing.

I can tell you're truly a good person. Where did you learn it all? What are your parents like? What was your university experience like? What activities did you take on as a boy? What's your favorite color?

I want to know!!

I want to know you.

xoxo
Michèle

PS You signed your Christmas card "I'll see you in the New Year." Is that a promise?

PPS And incidentally you're seven years older than I am. Don't push your luck, pal!

The chanter

When Bethany opens her front door, she feels nervous. She's worried that he'll think she's too dressed up, or dressed up at all. She has done her hair and put on lipstick. Her top is smart. She isn't nervous. She is really nervous. She doesn't know why. She isn't good at the kiss-kiss greeting thing. It just isn't the way with her or her family. They are physically undemonstrative, emotionally modest, hard-working, church-loving, community-loving—but not very good at the kiss-kiss thing.

She notices Padnavacca is wearing cool jeans. Normally he's dishevelled. He's shaved. He has on a nice blue shirt. A blazer—Bethany gets a charge out of that. He has a UK look to him. Not a hockey player look, not North American. She likes that. And he has an umbrella.

"It's wet outside," he says. There is nothing in his words to suggest this might be a date, but there is something in his manner that makes the words sound just a little nervous. Or perhaps she's imagining it. They set off to research the first pub on their list. It's raining. They're organizing a social event for all the trainees on their psychotherapy course. A spontaneous idea has become a plan. They both love rain.

Now Bethany is sitting in a traditional English pub. There's someone playing an accordion in the corner. There's a duck in a glass case and an old bike hanging from the ceiling. People are smoking. Bethany feels foreign here and she likes it. She's from Prince Edward Island, Canada, same as Anne of Green Gables, and she grew up in a town of seven hundred people—now she clutches onto her London pub guide. It's a huge volume. She likes that. This is the first pub on her list to research.

Padnavacca the Scottish Buddhist monk sits down right next to her. She thought he'd sit opposite, the other side of the table. He's a Buddhist after all, and a monk, or something like that, she's not quite sure what, she thinks he was ordained but that doesn't necessarily make him a monk, and Buddhists must be shy and floaty and flaky and ethereal—*transcending*—and he has just said "we live", which must be a reference to his girlfriend, or wife, or lover, a way of signalling to Bethany that he is attached. They are not here on a date after all. Or are they?

They're studying together. They share the same supervisor. They've talked about their client work together. They've felt exposed, and familiar, and personal, but now so very unknown.

Bethany likes the way Padnavacca talks about clients. He's not judgemental. He's warm and accepting. He gives them space. He's emotionally aware. He's able to talk about a feeling, name it, play with it. She's a woman of science. He uses metaphors.

"It's such a coincidence we live five minutes from you," he says, using the plural, so she knows not to open up, even though he is sitting right there next to her, when he might have chosen to sit opposite. He has greenish eyes, fair skin, brown hair. He may be a Buddhist but he's Scottish.

Bethany is a MacDonald.

"We swim at the same pool," he says.

There's a family at the next table having supper with their grandmother. Bethany likes this pub. She's happy to stick with this one, no need to move on. There are no pubs where she grew up, no cafes to hang out, no nice clothes shops, nowhere to go out for dinner, nowhere to date—but this is not a date. It's easy talking with Padnavacca. She's forgotten her nerves. They talk and talk and talk. They talk about where they're from, their ambitions, their independence, their love of exercise, mental and physical. They both have damaged joints from too much running. They were both born in the same year. Maybe it's because of the accordion player, she's not aware how it happens, but Bethany tells Padnavacca about the bagpipes.

"The first time I played it was a kind of joke," she says. "I was ten years old. My grandfather thought figure skating was useless. He said he'd buy a set of pipes for anyone who could play. They're expensive. OK. So now I have bagpipes and I can play. I love playing. Of course I left them behind in Canada. I don't really play in the city anyway because the neighbourhood doesn't appreciate it."

Padnavacca laughs so hard he says it hurts. He can't believe it. His father is really serious about bagpipes. He's been playing for more than forty years. He teaches. He even makes his own reeds.

"You need a chanter so you can practise."

Canadian Bethany feels like she has come home.

It's getting towards closing time. The publican is doing that English pub thing, announcing, *Hurry up please it's time, come on, finish up please folks, hurry up please it's time.* The accordion player has stopped. Bethany is not sure when. The door is open. The lights are on.

Padnavacca suddenly says: "I'm interested in you. I'm into you." It's a little wild. "I'd like to be able to let you in."

"I like you too," Bethany says.

At this point she knows it's a date. It's nice to have that much clear. They kiss. A peck on the lips.

He walks her home. They kiss again, at her house, with passion. Bethany likes the way he kisses. He stays the night. They don't do anything but talk about Scotland and London and friends and life and how he shares his house with other Buddhists, not a girlfriend, and how he is not a monk or a priest at all, but he has lived without women for eight years (transcending, extreme)—until they fall asleep.

The next day they walk around the local park in sunshine—*their* local park—how many coffees do they have? Kids are playing ball. Adults are basking, or being walked by their dogs. Holding hands, Bethany and Padnavacca wander to the Victorian cemetery down the road, all mossy mounds and ivy tangles and broken-winged angels, enjoying the soft light as it slants on narrow paths, discovering the abandoned church that hides in the centre like a secret in a forest, pigeons clapping through its glassless windows.

Bethany and Padnavacca talk and talk and talk. They talk until they're tired. They both have homework to do, papers to write.

"I'm not good at that kiss-kiss thing," she says. "So maybe you can help me with that?"

He does.

We should talk before weds, he texts her later.

So they do. It's the first time Bethany hears his voice on the phone. It's gentle, lovely. It ought to be. His Buddhist name, given to him by another priest, or monk, means 'lotus voice'. It's auspicious and beautiful.

Wednesday is the regular session with their supervisor. They worry she'll catch on, that maybe their emotions will interfere with their work. They feel like naughty kids with a secret. They arrange to meet in a few days' time but they can't wait. They meet for tea. (They've met once for tea, before the date that was not a date, a Canadian-style tea-and-cookies drop-in, a casual distraction from the dissertation, which left her feeling alive and good, like she'd found a new friend, just a friend—although she had noticed the contours of his body, a glimpse of his stomach, nice strong legs.)

Next thing she knows, he's going to Scotland. That's where his parents are. They call him James. It's the name they gave him after all, or before all.

Bethany has lots of revision to do anyway. She has a degree to get.

He takes the train.

There were no trains where Bethany grew up. Back home in her small town, where everything is quaint and local, where the tourist industry depends on an adorable but defiant literary orphan called Anne of Green Gables, where real lives are tightly enmeshed and the community is close-knit, where humanities subjects are pastimes, where to be 'driven' is to be difficult, where you get married and have kids—back home is where Bethany's ex-husband lives. He's a big softie, a football player, a teacher, a good person. She'd been with him since she was fifteen. He was like a brother. The very thought of splitting up with him was nauseating. They came to London together. He hated it; she loved it. Her psychotherapy course was the force that finally split them. She was in therapy as part of her training, so the truth was in her face. He went back home. She's been single now for more than three years and the divorce is on its way. She's about to graduate. Back home in her small town, everyone still asks, assuming, *When are you returning?*

Padnavacca texts her. He's twelve miles or so from Edinburgh. When is he returning?

Hey lovely. Me in a green & windy wheat field, whoosh. Big blue sky & fluffy clouds. Wee yellow flowers 2. I'm just gonna lie here & send you good vibes. XX :)

She saves the message to her archive. His wishes help her study.

He texts her from the train as it rushes back towards England from Scotland.

Clickety clack woo woo clickety clack whoosh woo!! Me absolutely WHIZZING 2wards you. On schedule so far 4 Kings X @ 9.43 :) :) :) XXX

She goes to the station to meet him. Inside the stop-start loops of traffic, behind the mess of building works and shops and hoardings, it's a grand old sprawl of architecture from the days of the Great Northern Railway. There are people everywhere, so many. Tunnels and stairways and concourses. The platform is cold and bright under a fragile roof of old white glass. The train board says *Edinburgh Waverley*. Bethany gets a charge out of that. When the train pulls in, she searches the crowd and every head is his, every face is his, every man and woman, every fat and thin and in-between body becomes his well-built muscular lean-fit body walking towards her.

Then she sees him. He walks towards her with that UK look, not the North American hockey player look.

"Nobody's ever met me at the train before," he says when he is close. There are tears in his eyes.

"I've brought you a present," he says.

Later, he takes something out of his backpack. It's a cylinder, like a spaghetti tin, or a tube for keeping knitting needles, wrapped in wild '70s fabric. It's beautiful.

"Now you can practise," Padnavacca says, as Bethany takes her gift out of the tin.

"My father made it for you."

Like a miniature instrument without bag or drones, this chanter is a quirky mix of other old chanter parts salvaged and grafted together, yellowed ivory on the bottom piece, some nickel trim, different kinds of wood, a plastic mouthpiece in two parts with black tape at the base. It has lots of texture and much more meaning than a regular chanter from a store. And it was made for her. Bethany runs her fingers along the indented words on one part: *GRAINGER & CAMPBELL, GLASGOW*—her new instrument has Scotland all over it. She can practise now, learn her tunes quietly, without feeling like she ought to be shut away in a garage. In fact, she's feeling a bit prouder of being a piper these days. It's beginning to feel interesting and accessible.

"You must come to Scotland with me, get in touch with your MacDonald side," Padnavacca smiles.

Bethany loves his smile. It's wide and generous.

"And meet my parents—you've already got an 'in' with my father and he's a hard man to please."

"And what about your mother?" Bethany asks, half

joking. She's looking forward to Scotland, to meeting his parents. It feels right and fitting.

"My mother used this tin to hold her needles," Padnavacca says. "She likes knitting."

"I love to knit!" Bethany laughs. It's the happy truth.

One all

She can always hear the growl of his motorbike. It's a single sound within the roar of traffic, as distinct as a personal voice in a crowd. She knows he is approaching long before he appears.

His saddle of choice is a sit-up-and-beg Harley-Davidson. He enjoys rumbling along in black on black. He bare-faces the wind, narrowing his blonde-lashed eyes. His white arms are wrapped in black tattoos.

She rides a sports bike. She wears a beautiful full-face helmet that matches her machine. She leans forward into the wind like an enamelled insect. She goes fast, very fast. It's an aesthetic experience, colourful, streamlined.

She's at home in the country.

He's a city boy, through and through.

She's an entrepreneur, a consultant who has systematized everything from airports to hospitals. She is addicted to work, works all the hours, will work for ever.

He has worked hard to achieve the earliest possible semi-retirement. He used to run a company; now he does a bit of work, a lot of biking.

They are both forty-nine.

They both love football.

"Life would be so much easier if you were an Arsenal fan," she says.

"If I'd been an Arsenal fan, we'd never have met," he says.

Four years ago Sam was in enemy territory. She was the one and only Arsenal fan in a Manchester pub full of United fans. Arsenal had won, away from home, conquered the enemy on their home turf. Not just the match. The Premiership. Sam was high with victory. She had spent the game sitting in an enemy seat, thanks to her friend and colleague Malcolm—he couldn't help it if he supported the wrong team. (They had worked out a system: she would get him to matches at Highbury; he would get her to matches at Old Trafford.)

Sam had never known a mismatch like today: she'd been surrounded by people cheering at the worst time, groaning inappropriately, disagreeing with all the right decisions. Everything was topsy-turvy. It was worse than wanting to laugh at a funeral. She'd suppressed the energy of her cheers by throwing her arms down and pretending to tie her shoelaces, when really she should have been letting herself go, jumping into the air and shrieking.

Now here she was in the pub with the other side's crowd. Malcolm was gloomy, Sam almost dizzy with the suppression of her joy. It was a kind of ecstasy that thrilled through her blood.

"I'm buying a drink for everybody," she announced.

They seemed willing enough. They needed consolation.

"No thanks," one United fan said. "I'm not in your round."

"We've just won the league at Old Trafford, so you're *all* in my round!"

"Oh go on then," the stranger said.

He was cute. He had baby eyes, bright blue, open. They drew her in.

"What's a nice gunner like you doing in a place like this?" He seemed fairly relaxed for someone on the losing side.

"Celebrating our win," she said, gloating.

After the round was sorted, thirty-five drinks in all, she noticed him again, sitting at the bar, flirting and enjoying other people.

"Who's that person smiling?" she asked Malcolm casually.

"That's Fergus," Malcolm said. "He's always smiling."

Later, on the train back to London, they ended up together, three of them at the same table. Malcolm, Fergus and Sam. Every carriage was full of fans. Inconsolable Manchester United fans, celebratory Arsenal fans. She was sitting with the enemy. The train pulled out of Manchester Piccadilly station and was just past Stockport, hardly any distance, when Fergus stood up and offered to get coffee. Further down the train someone was giving away free drinks, kissing Arsenal supporters, handing out beers by the case.

Fergus didn't return until after Milton Keynes, an hour and a half later. He was everybody's friend. The coffee was lukewarm.

"Sorry," he grinned. "No milk or sugar. I got waylaid."

"No problem," said Sam. "Malcolm and I managed OK without you."

At London Euston, they all said goodbye, and Sam went home, fuzzy with euphoria. She tingled. The world was beautiful. She could hardly believe it. Arsenal had won the Premiership at Old Trafford. It was the best feeling of her life.

A year or so later, Malcolm was organizing a party to celebrate an industry award for work he'd done with Sam. She'd been instrumental in his success. He drew up a list of guests, work contacts, football fans and neighbours.

"Who else can we invite?" he asked her.

"Fergus is good for a laugh," Sam said.

At the party, Malcolm's neighbours seemed to know all about her. It was almost like meeting the family. Why had he been praising her so much? She was flattered and surprised. After a banquet lunch, everyone fell into a local pub and drank champagne until dark. They filled the place with their noise. Someone smuggled in giant takeaway tubs of fried chicken, which troubled the publican but added to the group hilarity.

A glamorous woman leaned against the bar and flirted with Fergus. She was wearing a beautiful dress with straps designed to be eaten off her shoulders—or so Sam thought she heard her say. Fergus didn't seem to be too interested.

"Cheers to the enemy!" he said to Sam.

She had to raise her voice to be clear in the clamour. "How long have you been into Man U?"

"You mean Man United."

"OK, Man United then."

"Forty years. I've been travelling up on that train for thirty-six. You?"

"It's written into my system. My ex was one of the Highbury doctors. We lived in the shadow of the ground."

"My condolences," Fergus smiled.

"Everyone here is mad about football," the woman in the dress said to Fergus. She played her fingers over her straps. "Tell me, why do you love your team?"

Fergus drained his glass, straightened up and declared his love to both women: "We play open, attractive football. We're entertaining, good to watch. We play to win, and we usually do."

Why did everything sound ambiguous?

Sam laughed. "Are you talking about your team or what?"

"We have a huge global following—"

"They've got a huge amount of money!" Sam said.

Fergus leaned towards the woman and pointed at Sam. "Whereas our competitors, as supported by present company—"

"Don't you dare say Arsenal are boring!"

"Our competitors," Fergus ignored Sam's interruption, "like to win games one nil."

"It's hard to get a goal past our defenders," Sam said. "But our game's changed. We're different now. We use the whole field. We play to score."

"Cheers to that," Fergus grinned, raising his empty glass.

When Sam was ready to leave the party at last, Malcolm gave her a wrapped gift.

"Thanks for everything," he said. "I couldn't have done it without you."

"You're the winner," said Sam, and kissed his cheek.

She was halfway home, walking, when she peeled off the paper and opened the box. Inside was a framed photograph of the Arsenal team, signed personally by her favourite player: *To Sam, love Freddie XXX*. She felt her heart skip a beat. It was so thoughtful, so magnanimous. Malcolm was a Man United fan after all. He had written on the back: *Here's to teamwork! love Malcolm XXX*. She decided to go back and thank him properly.

She found him talking to Fergus outside the pub. Everyone was waiting for taxis, standing about in darkness and street light, tipsy.

Sam gave Malcolm a warm hug.

"It's beautiful," she said quietly. "Thank you. I'm really touched."

Malcolm hesitated, as if he was about to say something.

"Hey, here's your taxi." Fergus waved a black cab over.

"Goodnight," Malcolm said.

Sam watched as the car drove away.

"I thought you'd gone," said Fergus.

"I was halfway home but I remembered something."

"I thought you were with Malcolm," he said.

"He's very dear to me."

"Every time I see you, you're with him."

"He's a good friend."

"Mine too," Fergus said. "I'll walk you back."

They walked home the long way. At her door they kissed.

Four Premierships later …

"After our first date I felt high, though not as high as an Arsenal win. A different feeling," Sam says. "And after our first night together I remember waking up in blazing sunshine with the blast of traffic outside the window—I was late for work! I dressed in a rush, jumped in a cab and raced all the way. When I got home, he'd bought groceries and washing powder because I'd run out—such an ordinary thing, but it felt nice. We had dinner together. We discovered we shared a passion for motorbikes, even though we had a different passion in common." Sam shrugs philosophically. "He's a Harley man."

"She likes sports racers."

"He stayed the next night, and the next."

"Manchester United vs Arsenal. I called it sleeping with the enemy. When we talked about the next game I said to her: I hope you lose."

"And I said I hope you draw."

"So I said, OK, I hope you draw."

"He negotiates!" Sam says. "He's caring, giving and embracing, but he's nobody's pup. I learn something new about him every day. He's worked me out and he's all right. He brings out the best in me. It took me all this time to know what I wanted."

"She's done so many things," says Fergus. "She has such a great appetite for life. She's happy to jump on the back of a bike for three thousand miles. She's bright, she's attractive, she's brave." He frowns. "But she loves the morning."

"Whereas he lives by night," she says. "We've learned to do things in the early evening!"

"She has a posh seat at the game. I buy normal tickets."

"I'm planning to do a PhD on how the price of a football ticket has changed over time, compared with a newspaper round."

"She spends."

"He saves."

"I was single for three years," Fergus says. "And happy."

"Me too. Three years. Happy."

"We have so much in common!" says Fergus.

"We both love motorbikes," says Sam.

"And football."

"Despite our differences."

"We've talked about marriage. I said we could get married if it would make her happy. She got annoyed."

Sam looks heavenwards. "You should want to get married to make yourself happy, not just to please me."

"You should be happy I'd do it to make you happy—"

"We manage in the off-season!"

Hungarian kiss

Vilmos arrived at Victoria station. He had travelled by train, and train, and ferry, and train, all the way from Hungary. It was 1963. He was nineteen years old and ready for the world. He was wearing pointed shoes, a suit with a tightly knotted tie, a jaunty hat with a feather in it. He couldn't speak English. London crashed upon him with its fabulous populous clutter. He'd never felt anything like it. He had never been anywhere before, only small places, poor places. Places emptied of Jews. Places porous enough to absorb Jews.

Vilmos looked for his uncle Imre.

He had seen him only once before, a long time ago, waving across No Man's Land. The guards, in a casual moment, had allowed Vilmos to walk underneath the barrier for a while. He was only four years old and his uncle was the image of a wise old man even then, but the image was confined to another country, distant. The memory now was still fresh as a photograph in Vilmos's mind, captured in an instant.

And there he was again, the sage in the crowd, elderly, distinctive, waving, familiar, come to collect him from Victoria station, unfamiliar. Uncle Imre kissed him on both cheeks, *puszi*, *puszi*, and they made their way back to his apartment in a taxi. The roads were huge and crammed with vehicles, red buses two storeys high, blacks, Indians, men with long hair, palaces. Vilmos and his uncle spoke Hungarian together. Vilmos passed on his mother's regards. All her other siblings had died or dispersed. She had planned this London trip to help secure her only child's future. It mattered to her more than anything else in the world, Vilmos knew that. He was bonded to her beyond borders.

Uncle Imre lived like a king on Park Lane. There was a concierge and an automatic lift that took them all the way to the sixth floor. There was a very long corridor. Everything was strange, like images from a film, or descriptions in a book. Kati opened the door. She was wearing make-up; the simple fact of it was striking, excessive. She was pretty. She came out into the corridor, holding an infant.

"Her name is Pearl," Kati smiled. "But we call her *Angyalom. Kis bogaram. Puszi.*"

The Hungarian words for angel, my little bug, kiss—not the kind of kiss that lovers give, but the kiss of affection, welcome, cosy warmth. Vilmos instantly felt those things for Pearl. She was adorable and she knew it.

"Come in, come in," Kati invited Vilmos. A kiss on each cheek.

He caught a glimpse of himself in the mirror of her eyes: a young man with the stamp of poor Eastern Europe all over him. Here was the woman who had roamed the world with his old uncle. They had written to him from New York, Capri, Athens, Monte Carlo, Paris ... Vilmos had loved and collected their postcards, gazed at images of skyscrapers and parasol pines, monuments and neon signs. He'd kept them safely in a wooden box. There was a whiff of worldliness in their layers.

Here was Kati who had been on the telephone from London once. A call from London was special. It was costly and difficult, a complicated connection. Pregnant Kati had spoken a few words and suddenly muttered "just a minute" before Uncle Imre had taken over: "Sorry, she had to rush off to be sick."

That was Pearl inside her, the baby to be born out of wedlock, conceived out of love and desire. Vilmos hadn't much experience of love or desire.

Within a day he felt at home in his new home, even though his family of strangers was so foreign to him. Uncle and Kati managed a secretarial services company together. They worked sixteen hours a day. Uncle already had a wife (his third) at another address, but he'd never had a child before. He lived in the Park Lane apartment three nights a week. It was not a happy arrangement. And little Pearl scampered about like a rabbit.

Vilmos fell into being Pearl's second father. He was young, he loved her and he was there for her. He would hold her, teach her, cajole her when she needed persuading, play with her when she needed distraction. Vilmos knew all about stepfathering. His own father, whom he'd never seen, had been taken away to a work camp, and then a concentration camp.

In 1945, a random Russian stopped his truck on the road out of Hungary, to pick up the poor woman holding her tiny baby and dangling her gold watch in the air. (She kept her husband's gold watch tucked into her clothes.) Truck drivers were partial to watches—some of them had ten on one arm. A random Romanian policeman helped mother and child off the truck at the border. Vilmos had escaped the bombs, the exterminators and the hunger. Within months of his birth, a Transylvanian border town became his new home. And the Romanian policeman became his stepfather.

Vilmos kept his father's gold watch. He wore it to London.

He applied himself to learning English. He spent three months studying until he gained his certificate. He felt proud. He could speak the language almost like a local. He dreamed of being an actor, but drama school turned him down. What kind of actor? He didn't know. He had worked in a Romanian theatre. He started studying photography instead.

"I wanted to be an actress," Kati said to Vilmos. "My father was an actor." She pointed at the beautiful oil painting that hung on her living room wall, the image of a handsome man refracted through angular facets of light and shade. Jewel colours.

"He played the lead role in Alexander Korda's big film about the House of Hapsburg, a silent movie, made the year before I was born," Kati said. Her eyes were green-grey. She adored the young man in the portrait who was her father.

Vilmos was impressed. The Hungarian director had launched and built film empires in his home country, America and Britain.

"The film was so successful, Korda went to Hollywood and invited my father over," Kati said. "But my father chose to stay in Budapest and play his part in the local theatre, a kind of musical. *Business is a dirty word in this family*, he said. He had no business sense. They could have sold him and he'd know nothing about it!"

Vilmos could see something of Kati in the portrait, the clarity in the eyes, the honest, fearless self-belief.

"He was intelligent, a liberal like my Imre, but he was no good at business, unlike my Imre." Kati smiled. "And of course, because he chose to stay put, he ended up everywhere. He was interned in Wales, where they taught him English and bridge, wounded at the Front, imprisoned in Russia, escaped back to Hungary via Manchuria …"

Vilmos could hear the world in her, the world he had not yet seen. This was Kati of the postcards and the international phone call, the young wife of an old Pole who'd escaped France on the last ship when World War Two broke, the young widow who fell in love with old Imre of Hungary, Italy, New York and London.

Imre had courted penniless Kati instead of hiring her as a secretary. She'd turned up for her interview, rain splashed and tear prone. He'd sat with his back to her, hunched over a typewriter, barely turning to look at her, while his colleagues asked her questions. Now he spent so much time away from her, away from home, it seemed as if he barely turned to look at her again.

Kati was miserable, lonely. Life felt difficult, complicated. When she came home from work, her darling Pearl was already asleep. There was only Vilmos. She needed a shoulder to cry on. She cried on his shoulder.

Vilmos started to fall in love. It was a gradual feeling, reactive, tentative, not decided. She was double his age. He could not betray his benefactor, his mother's brother.

He photographed Kati's intelligent green-grey eyes, her soft skin, the waves of her brown hair, her long heart-shaped face. He admired her through the camera lens, and then without shutters. He captured her. They kissed.

Csok, the Hungarian word for a grown-up kiss, the kiss that lovers give, full of desire. It felt wrong, but it felt natural.

"I think the world of you," Vilmos said. "You are the Goddess Kati, my goddess, *isteni.*"

Little kisses, soft skin, adoring kisses, gazing kisses, lingering, passionate kisses, harmony, devotion. It was a secret. Their secret. A closeted love, behind closed doors. It felt natural, but it felt wrong.

Imre divorced his third wife and agreed to make Kati his fourth. Little Pearl was three years old by then. The marriage was for her sake.

Vilmos sat in the wedding car that collected Kati from the hairdresser's. She was about to get married, but not to him.

"At the hairdresser's, I said I'm going to a wedding, will you make my hair nice?" Kati told him later. "I never said it was *my* wedding."

Vilmos became disagreeable, abrasive. He behaved like an obnoxious teenager. Hurtful, reckless, free. He was trying to create emotional distance, but it didn't work. When his visa expired, he prepared to move out, to return to Hungary. At least there would be physical distance.

"You've escaped once already," Kati cried. "You won't be so lucky twice. Don't go back. You'll never get out again."

She was wrong and he was lucky. He escaped Hungary for the second time, before the Russians marched into Prague in 1968. He couldn't wait to get back to England. London was his home now, because Kati was his heart.

So he returned to live on Park Lane with his adopted family: his part-time uncle, his surrogate daughter and his mistress-aunt. He finished his photography diploma and Uncle Imre appointed him co-director of the family business, to keep him in England when his student visa expired. Imre, Kati and

Vilmos shared a home and a company, year after year. Their love was never discussed.

When Imre died at seventy-four, skiing in Switzerland, Vilmos was not yet thirty. He inherited the grave responsibility of family, business and his uncle's extravagant debts. He had to work hard. But he had Kati to himself at last. And the truth could out. Slowly, slowly, inch by inch, they crossed the borders, revealed their love to the outside world, took on a new identity.

More than forty years later, they are still together (but not on Park Lane). Faithful, devoted, unmarried, inseparable.

"And here comes the age difference," Kati smiles. "Pearl recently said to me: *What happened to you, mummy? You used to be such a trendy chick!* I am nearly eighty-two years old and Vilmos is sixty-two. My priorities are different."

Vilmos can dash about London on a bicycle but Kati has felt the physical frailty of age.

"People must have seen and formed an opinion," she reflects. "And not necessarily the kindest. His mother is still not happy about it. There is an exceptional tie between them. Having lost everyone except him, having escaped with her little baby to another country, he was the one person who was entirely her own. Now he goes back there to see her every year for birthdays. She still doesn't accept who I am … But when you think about our life, our romance was almost inevitable."

"It has been a gradual process," says Vilmos. "Gradually increasing. It has never stopped increasing. There's no point talking about me, or her. There's just us."

Puszi. Csok. And all the other kisses in between.

New York, London IV

Michèle,

My God what a voice you have! Your package was on the shelf at the bottom of the stairs as I walked out to work—I opened it in my car and put the tape on. I was tired—I'd been on call all night—you started singing in such a strong confident voice—I turned it right up and played both songs as I drove into work and I swear the hair on my neck stood up and I got that tingle in my spine that comes I don't know why but it does when something is good and touches me. You have so many voices—nuances in your voice from soft and vulnerable to full and open and cool and sassy—I especially liked the second song—I don't know the original version but I don't think I need to hear it!

Where are you sending this tape? You must send it everywhere—I am really so impressed. I read your letter when I got to work—your novel! You paint vivid pictures of your family—you never say obvious things about them but offer snapshots of their traits and attitudes, which makes for real reading. I love the energy of your writing.

It is late at night—I've been hectic the last couple of days—wanting to write straight back. The people I had in court on the day I received your letter got a great deal—I was buzzed up again and feeling good about life—full of energy and vitality with the words of my speeches to the court flowing.

What a coy sweetie you were at 2½—the picture was a brilliant idea! I presume those are your sisters in the background. I haven't got any photos of me at 2½. I found one of me getting my hair cut. I've had long hair nearly all my life—the moment caught in this photo is the moment it all came off.

Michèle,

How do I start? First—thank you for the wonderful tape—I got back from a hard day at court and put it on my walkman, put my feet up on the table not being quite sure what to expect—about an hour later with a completely dead right leg I got up with a big smile on my face. It was good to hear you talking, your voice, your intonations and your ideas flowing out—it was strangely intimate and yet I kept wanting to join in. Like you, the last few weeks have been hectic and difficult—I have thought of you often and heard your voice—there have been times when I've wanted you around to see what you'd think or feel—there was an incredible full moon last night—maybe that's what picked me up again!

I've been working too hard and partying too hard—which is fun and exhilarating but sort of ultimately unsatisfying. I've been violently independent and single—flirting and such, then disappearing into my own space again. Your words about not making yourself vulnerable to people or things ring very true—I won't waste time on stupid relationships or pointless liaisons.

It's spring time here. It hasn't rained for ages, which is incredible. I love this time of year—new growth—I feel like you about winter. It is a hibernation time. Autumn is beautiful and colourful but it just descends into bleakness until the sun shines again—getting my dusty surfboard out and crashing about in big blue-green waves, sitting out afterwards with friends drinking beer and being silly—you just can't do it in winter!

I don't know the books you mention—or I don't think I do. I'll look them up. It's funny, I just saw the end of '84 Charing Cross Road'—the film—the other day about two people writing to each other for years and years but never meeting, drawn by their obsession with literature and ideas—then, two days later, you talk of reading—I hope we meet before I die!! They didn't manage to! I didn't see the first hour or so, so I don't know how it started—in a bookshop I think—not quite a jazz gig!

I've just had a little jump around my room—I love dancing.

New York, London IV

Your correspondence still gives me such a buzz—I love it—it's such a special thing—keep singing.

Love
Marcus
XX

What the heart chooses

~ ~

Zhen Zhu looked up at the huge sky above her head and said: "I'm not greedy. I just want one person. The world is so big and there are so many people, but I only want one. I want to feel safe and happy with someone." She felt so lonely. There was nothing for her to live for, except her daughter.

Lucky Aunt Phoenix

One week later, Auntie Feng was launching a new Chinese restaurant. For the opening night she invited everyone she knew. Her friends, her neighbours, her acupuncturist, even her postman, would eat together and celebrate. She called Zhen Zhu to ask if she'd help with the work.

Zhen Zhu lived in a different city. She was studying English and waitressing part-time. She wanted to give her aunt a hand, but it was unlikely that she would get away from her own work, so she said no. When her shift was changed at the last minute, she decided to just turn up.

She caught a train. She sat and watched her solitary face in reflection, a ghost scudding past the darkened landscape, translucent as a tissue-paper mask. She looked away. There were chips and greasy wrappings left on the upholstered seats. A discarded newspaper, open-flapped to reveal a photo of a young woman, blonde and topless. Initials scratched and scrawled on glass and plastic.

Zhen Zhu felt the train hurtle into the night and part of her wished it would not stop. Everything would be easier if the train did not stop. She could just continue to sit there, going somewhere, being purposeful, doing nothing but living one moment at a time.

Outside, the June air was warm and humid, almost tropical. On nights like this Zhen Zhu was reminded of Hong Kong. She could smell garlic. And damp decay. She looked for the rabbit in the moon, but she could not see it. The street was bright with the lights of *Feng Dim Sum*, fringes of gold bunting, red and white bulbs strung across the window, flashing like English Christmas.

Before going inside, Zhen Zhu tied back her long, thick hair. The place was full of people, as cheerful and noisy as a popular restaurant back home, not one spare seat or table. The walls were shiny with fresh paint, and the fancy phoenix lamps Auntie Feng had imported from China gave off a clear white light. Everything was brand new.

Auntie was pleased and surprised to see her. The banquet was starting.

"Look how many people!" she said. "We needed you."

She introduced Zhen Zhu to the other two waitresses, Ushi and Wei. Together they drew up a new table allocation and Zhen Zhu started work on her section, taking orders and serving. She was stacking bamboo boxes full of steamed dumplings when she heard Ushi call her over to help.

"I'll take these," Auntie said. "You look after that table. The one in the dark shirt is my acupuncturist and also my friend. Give him special treatment."

Zhen Zhu went over. There were two men, both English, one plum shirt, one white shirt.

"I don't know what he's talking about," Ushi whispered in Cantonese. "My English isn't good like yours."

"I wanted to know if there was any monosodium glutamate in the food," the Englishman in the plum shirt was saying, slowly and politely. "I know it's a set menu, but I can't eat monosodium glutamate."

Zhen Zhu translated for Ushi and reassured the customer. "I'm sure we can prepare special dishes for you without MSG."

"And I'm vegetarian," he added.

Ushi looked perplexed by that word too.

The other Englishman smiled.

"No problem," Zhen Zhu smiled.

"How are you?" the other Englishman asked her in Cantonese. The question was improbable and his accent almost unintelligible.

"I am very well, thank you," Zhen Zhu replied in Cantonese. "Where did you learn to speak the language?"

"Canton City. Guangzhou."

He understood, then. He wasn't just parroting phrases.

"My name is Martin," he persevered in translation. "I teach kung fu. My friend is an acupuncturist. I am studying to be an acupuncturist. My friend is an acupuncturist for your aunt." He had a friendly face. Big slate-blue eyes with thick black lashes.

"Hello Martin, the kung fu teacher student acupuncturist with the acupuncturist friend," said Zhen Zhu in Cantonese, feeling cheeky. "I hope you enjoy the food."

"I hope you have ..." Martin frowned, paused and fell

into English. "Toffee banana with ice cream. It's my favourite."

"We have vegetarian toffee banana with ice cream, no MSG, but what about some dinner first?" Zhen Zhu scribbled earnestly in her order book to offset the mischief in her voice.

She took the acupuncturists' order, turned and headed for the kitchen.

"You can look after that table," Auntie Feng said to her on the way. "Swap with Ushi. Take care of them."

Zhen Zhu was holding four heavy sizzling griddles, when Martin asked for her phone number.

She was used to this. It happened all the time. English men often asked Chinese waitresses for their phone numbers. His face seemed very kind, but English men had different ideas about girls and dates. They weren't serious. They were used to one-night stands, so different from Chinese culture. She didn't want to waste her time. It was not difficult to meet men, but it was difficult to meet real love.

"The number is on the menu," Zhen Zhu said, still bearing the weight of the sizzling griddles. She could feel her face absorbing the salty steam. She could feel a drop of sweat as it trickled, tickled, down the curve of her back. Her forearms were beginning to ache.

He was younger, she could see that, inauspicious. Twenty-something. She was thirty-two and had an eight-year-old daughter.

"These dishes are losing their sizzle," she said in Cantonese. "But they're gaining in weight!"

She moved on to the next table and served. As she passed Martin, he asked for her number again.

"Just a moment," Zhen Zhu said.

She returned with a menu in her hand. *Feng Dim Sum*. She pointed at the back. Auntie had commissioned a traditional calligrapher to paint the characters. The brush strokes were black on white, dancing like long hair in the wind. *Feng* meant phoenix. *Dim sum* meant more than food. *Touch the heart. What your heart chooses.* But it was the phone number she wanted Martin to read.

"The number is there," she said, in English. "Seven days a week."

"I need some language help," he said. "Maybe we can swap. You teach me Chinese, I learn English?"

Zhen Zhu thought for a second, then laughed.

"Nobody ever understands what I'm saying when I speak Cantonese." Martin spoke in English now. "I practise whenever I can, but you're the first person I've met who seems to understand me!"

Zhen Zhu did not say that she was used to her daughter's accent—it was the accent of an eight-year-old with an English flavour despite Chinese Sunday school.

She told her aunt about the customer's special request.

"Give him what he wants," Auntie Feng said. "Even if it's not on the set menu."

Zhen Zhu wanted to laugh. When she returned with two indulgent desserts, she gave Martin her phone number. She was studying English and her conversation skills needed to improve after all these years.

White crane style

The next morning Martin called Zhen Zhu's number. He phoned at eight o'clock. There was no answer. He didn't leave a message. He kept calling. Finally, in the afternoon, she answered.

She had a charming voice, melodious and gentle. He pictured her face, so full of light that he remembered it now as being almost transparent. Her eyes had shone as brightly as eyes through tears.

"I'm going to visit my granddad, so I'm passing by your way. Can you meet me for a drink?" He'd planned to say it in Cantonese but he didn't want to push his luck.

She agreed.

He wore the white silk shirt he'd bought in China. He picked up his language book and took it with him.

They met at the pub on the lake's edge. It was a mild June day with the fresh green clarity of early summer. Families navigated the curling paths of the grass labyrinth. Others lingered at the peace pagoda. Water birds waded in the shallows or swam through the air—grey herons, terns, lapwings, plovers.

Zhen Zhu looked lovely. Her hair was out. She had a beautiful smile. She was ready to practise her English, and help him with his Cantonese. They shared the language book.

"Why did you learn Chinese?" she asked.

"Ever since I was a boy I wanted to study kung fu. I was inspired by those films set in 'Old China', the Shaw brothers, early Jackie Chan. Five years ago I sold my car to pay for the trip and study crane-style kung fu with one of the best masters in Canton. It was weird for them having a foreigner there in 1990. It's still not that common. My teacher's a very famous kung fu master. He can't speak English, but we had a real bond, and we had an interpreter.

I was there for six months, sleeping on a wooden board, using a bucket and tap to wash, training for nine hours a day. At the end, my master said to me *you've got to learn Cantonese*. So I did, but it was only one or two years later that I felt I'd broken through, got into the philosophy and the spirit of it. I meant it when I said you're the first person who actually understands me—why is that?"

"I can understand you because of my daughter," Zhen Zhu said.

Martin hadn't expected this answer.

"You sound like her," Zhen Zhu said. "I was taking her to Chinese Sunday school when you phoned this morning. That's why I missed your calls. I'm a single mother."

"Is her father … alive?"

Zhen Zhu nodded. "I fell in love when I was sixteen. I was eighteen when we married, too young. I was one of eleven children and he paid me attention, made me feel special. He was living in England, so we left Hong Kong to live here together. He was violent. I did not know he would be violent. And he was a gambler. I didn't know that either. I thought having a child would change him, but it didn't. We were married for ten years. He was not good for me or for my daughter. I left him."

Martin was touched by her openness. It was disarming.

"When did you leave him?" he asked.

"Ruby was three. It was five years ago—the same time you went to Canton."

Martin suddenly noticed the buttons on Zhen Zhu's shirt. "Look!"

She read upside-down and blushed. "It must be the brand. I've never noticed that before."

Each bronze button was embossed with his name.

Lucky Aunt Two Swallows

Zhen Zhu had been meeting Martin for eight months. Each time he brought his book, and together they pored over writing and meaning and pronunciation. His accent and her fluency had improved. They fell in and out of both languages with ease.

Zhen Zhu liked him. He was always on time. He was very kind and thoughtful. He didn't throw away words. He seemed to understand her. They laughed. He talked about his pet rabbit, which ran free in the garden. Martin meditated *qigong* style and the rabbit would stand next to him in the same posture, upright, legs balanced, paws outstretched. Zhen Zhu always made a point of asking after the meditating rabbit. Martin was learning her language and she was learning how to love. But she felt guilty. She was a mother. She would not allow him to meet Ruby. He was English—her family did not approve. He was eight years younger, which was inauspicious. Such an age difference meant no longevity for the relationship, only transience—her family did not approve.

Until Auntie Yan Yan.

"He's nice!" she said to Zhen Zhu. "What are you waiting for?"

Auntie Yan Yan was visiting from Hong Kong. She had big wavy hair and a mole on her cheek like a beauty spot. She was as elegant as her name. She was a thousand years old, but she looked no more than forty.

"Inauspicious? Your uncle was older than me *and* he was Chinese and look what happened—we got divorced. So much for obeying custom! You've been married anyway, so you know what I mean, you've done that, it's history. Why don't you try it with this young English man? Even if nothing comes of it, at least you'll have some nice memories. He's patient. He's not out to take advantage. Why don't you try it?"

"Maybe he just likes me for the language practice."

"That ex of yours gambled with your self-esteem. It's time you won it back."

Zhen Zhu met Martin again at the pub by the lake, indoors by the gas fire. There was frost on the grass outside, thin crusts of ice on moonlit puddles.

"Your Cantonese is much better," she said in English. "I think other Chinese people will understand you now."

"I even dream in Cantonese!" Martin said, not in English. "You're a very good teacher."

"My sister wants me to emigrate, to be with her in Vancouver. I belong with her. Ever since I visited her, I've been thinking about moving. It's a beautiful city, great opportunities, a good place for Ruby to grow up."

"I thought you felt uncomfortable when you went there."

"I didn't belong with the luxury or the ostentation." She didn't say that she belonged with Martin—but her daughter mattered more than him, more than herself. And then she remembered Auntie Yan Yan's words. *Why don't you try it?*

Zhen Zhu looked into Martin's eyes. She had loved his eyes, ever since their first meeting. He was a martial arts fighter and yet he was the most gentle man she had ever known. He was young but he was an old soul. He was not an English man, he was a person. It was the person she loved, the person inside the skin.

"I'm not an easy-to-get-into-relationships person," she said.

"Nor am I."

"I love you," she said.

Martin took her hands in his.

"I like you very much," he replied. "But I might go to China tomorrow. I still have so much training to do. I can't commit to you. And you might be off to Vancouver anyway."

Zhen Zhu knew that Martin had spent his whole life dreaming of his martial arts centre, aiming to create in England the kind of school he'd had to go to China to find. She knew that he had no family help, no easy way in. She knew how focused he needed to be. He'd never been anything but honest about that.

But she wanted him to say he loved her. She thought she wasn't good enough.

Instead he said: "Why don't we just let things take their course?"

Two hearts beating

Martin liked Zhen Zhu, loved Zhen Zhu, but he was not an easy-to-get-into-relationships person. They went out together, ate and drank together, practised t'ai chi together, slept together, slept apart. He travelled to China to study, and returned. She visited Vancouver to see her sister, and returned. He met Ruby and Ruby liked him. They got on well.

Each year, on the anniversary of their first meeting, the two lovers met halfway between their two English cities.

"Do we want to go on for another year?" he asked her. It was like renewing a short-term contract.

He wanted to.

She wanted to.

He had opened his martial arts school, training in his garden by day and using a rented hall for evening classes. Zhen Zhu loved to watch him teach. She could watch him for hours. It was so peaceful.

Martin was saving up, little by little, to buy his own business property. But before that, he and Zhen Zhu moved in with each other, still without formal commitment. They bought a house together. Zhen Zhu was pregnant.

"I want one boy, one girl," she said. "I want twins. Ruby would love that."

"That's as likely as winning the lottery!" Martin said.

He was terrified of becoming a father and was just getting used to the idea when Zhen Zhu miscarried. It was six weeks into the pregnancy. He was devastated.

"I feel I still have a baby," Zhen Zhu cried. She was distracted, pale with sorrow. The tiniest details became significant. She scrutinized everything she'd eaten, everything she'd done or not done, blaming herself for causing this unbearable loss of life.

"I feel I still have a baby," she said to him, her eyes shining with tears.

He understood her unwillingness to let go. It was grief. Denial. He felt it like a knot.

Zhen Zhu went to see her doctor, full of guilt and questions.

Martin was treating one of his own patients in the acupuncture room when the phone rang.

"Excuse me," he said to the bare back mapped with copper needles. "I don't have a receptionist."

It was Zhen Zhu on the phone. She was at the clinic.

"They did a scan," she said. "I lost one baby, but there are two heartbeats!"

Two lucky love birds

In the Year of the Tiger, Zhen Zhu gave birth to two beautiful babies, a boy and a girl. They were given Chinese names and English names. Ruby adored her new sister and brother.

When the twins were four, Martin opened his new centre dedicated to authentic martial arts and acupuncture. Zhen Zhu helped him pay the mortgage, paint the halls, lay the flooring. They had no help from family. No sleep either. They decorated the walls with dancing lion heads and opened on New Year's Day.

Years later, they decided to marry, but they went on their honeymoon first. They didn't travel far. They hired a cabin in the forest and left the doors open. At breakfast, two squirrels ventured into the kitchen and sat with them, casually eating rich tea biscuits. Just outside the door, a crowd slowly gathered. Multicoloured wood ducks, dark green pheasants and two white swans stood there and placidly looked in, each bird poised and still and alert. Zhen Zhu thought of the meditating rabbit and laughed. She felt so happy she could not stop smiling.

Finally—after the children, after the honeymoon, and a decade after meeting—she married him.

I BELIEVE
IN

Map of love

Arden and Luke met at art school in Hull, where abandoned shipyards gaped at a grey North Sea. They crossed the Atlantic for a life in Manhattan, flying south to the Caribbean for their wedding in the US Virgin Isles. A security guard was their witness. His name was Walker. He took the wedding photos. They're all blurry.

For Arden and Luke, being in New York meant being tough and fit and hard. They entered marathons. They spent long hours working, extra hours training, competing, nurturing new friends and contacts, living life on the grid. There was no space for English reserve. Luke worked in construction and Arden worked in interior design—both making places for people to feel at home. They invested in their own loft apartment but their dream was destroyed by flooding. The roof fell when the rain fell, and washed away their labour. The wooden floors they had laid by hand turned to warps and waves. The landlord was a pirate. They lost all their money but they didn't lose their perspective: they were still alive, they had their health and they were in love. They resolved to move back to England for a fresh start, picking up where they'd left off, rediscovering old friends and building new careers. They wanted to have children. They were both ready at last. They announced the plan in postcards home.

London at first was a life in translation. Finding employment wasn't as easy as they'd expected. But they began to search out their way. They renovated their council flat and made it beautiful. They began to earn money. Arden had two miscarriages, painful as births, her waters breaking long before the right time. Luke's employers went into receivership. The couple shed tears together, but they celebrated twelve years of marriage. And every Valentine's Day. Their friends stood by them, glad to have them home.

Luke started a course to teach body control and fitness. Arden was pregnant again, for the third time. Week after precious week the baby grew inside her, swelling her small and slender frame to improbable proportions. Mother-to-be and father put ultrasound scans on the fridge door, the first photos of their new family life. The baby kept growing, and Arden kept growing around the baby. She could feel that this one was here to stay, although she knew not to presume. Month after precious month, the baby grew, and kept growing, and stayed.

Arden imagined that Luke was straying. Her heart said so, and yet her head said not. She'd read that pregnant women feel undesirable and become insecure. The parenting books and her confidantes told her so. Luke could hardly wait for the baby. He stroked the hull of her belly like a worshipper.

Eight months into the pregnancy, their friends threw a baby shower. After the champagne toasts and unwrappings, the bright mobiles and grandmotherly knits, the cooing and clapping, Luke confessed that he had been having an affair and it mattered to him more than he could say.

Arden was sick with shock. It was worse news than if he had died.

Her blood pressure lurched. At the hospital they told her she was at risk and the baby was at risk. She had extra appointments with the midwife, who tried to comfort her with the sorry fact that her situation was common.

At relationship counselling sessions, Luke tried to find the words. He spoke like a lost man. He wanted the baby but he didn't want a life with Arden. Or he didn't know what he wanted. He'd never felt love like this before. It was a revelation, a new horizon, a new life. He didn't know what to do.

Despite her pain and fury, Arden wanted to make the marriage work. She couldn't believe that twelve years of partnership could dissolve in just a few months. She wanted to keep the man she had married and loved. She wanted a father for her child. If she had foreseen his departure—

Weeks after the baby was born, Luke moved out to live with his lover.

Arden wanted to kill him, and kill herself.

"I was devastated," Arden says, "by when it happened, how it happened, and how fast … I wanted to end my life."

She was prescribed antidepressants, a slow kind of floating. The drugs were in her breast milk, which worried her, and they didn't stop her from feeling suicidal, but they calmed her—enough to be a first-time mother on her own in a council flat with a new-born baby and no work. She went to counselling. How could she ever be sure of her feelings again?

"But I look at this lovely boy asleep in my lap now ..."

She is holding Noah, her beautiful two-year-old, a sunny child despite his rocky start in the world. She strokes his fair hair. His thumb is in his mouth. The other soft sleepy hand clings to a floppy velour rabbit. He has a shiny star sticker on his T-shirt. It says *WELL DONE*. He put all his toys away today without being asked. His sneakers have reflectors in the soles, but the lights are not flashing now. They are only activated when he stamps his feet. This is a child who only stamps his feet to show off his reflectors.

"You know that story about Edison?" Arden says. "It took him years and years, 120 different light bulb ideas, before he got it right. And when he was asked how he felt about all those failures, he said they weren't failures, but steps to success." She speaks with the calm clarity of hindsight.

"At those awful times of change, if only you knew what was around the corner. You'd know it was all going to be worth it."

Noah is not the only source of her happiness. She has started work again, designing textiles and ceramics for an international trade fair. Her creativity has surged. And she has met someone.

"All that upset, and feeling I wanted to jump in front of a bus ... I was so lacking in confidence after what happened. I'd always seen my worth in my work, being an artist and so on. I wasn't working because I'd had a child. It was a triple hit: my body had changed, my life had changed, and I had a baby. Who would want me?"

Arden recovered her strength through internet dating. It was terrifying. She hadn't dated since college, and then it was always friends of friends, people she knew about. She'd never been on a blind date in her life.

"I met a few different people. Usually I would think *nice guy but . . .* I was basically single for two years, and then came Matthew. He marked me as a favourite. That means you get an email saying so. You usually look and think *No! No! Don't like me!* But this time I was surprised. He was so handsome, and when I read his profile I thought: *He's lovely. Why does he like me?*

"Internet profiles all seem to say the same thing—*I've got a wild side but I also like to sit on the sofa and stay in*—it's very hard to write about yourself. But there are plenty of attractive girls a lot younger than me, and men tend to go for younger women, especially if they want kids."

Matthew sent Arden a message: *I really like your profile but I'm not sure if you'll be interested in me.*

Arden studied his photograph. He had a handsome face but she could see some funny old curtains in the background. She noticed people's interiors—it was her job. Was he a web geek with bad taste?

She wrote back.

He replied. More worrying than the curtains, he didn't ask any questions.

There were three men emailing her at this time and talking about themselves. None of them were asking her about herself.

Men often don't ask questions, a friend said. *Give him a chance. You can't tell until you meet him.*

First meeting

"I wanted to talk on the phone first, but he refused, saying he was useless on the phone. This worried me, but I liked his honesty. He seemed to know who he was. We arranged our first date. We both adore film, so we met at the Curzon cinema in Soho.

"He seemed really scared. He'd been registered online for just two weeks and only because his friend had suggested it. He hadn't dated anyone else. He hadn't even marked anyone else as a favourite. He'd chosen *atheist* as one of his preferences and got me, even though I'm agnostic. I was his first date and it was love at first sight! He was quiet and understated but also open and enthusiastic. He kept saying: *This is my first date—what are the odds of that?* He was saying it with his eyes and everything.

"We went to dinner. We talked about films, our kids, our families and friends, our marriages … He and his wife had been to relationship counselling for two years before they realized it was the only thing keeping them together. He didn't know anyone who was divorced. It took him a long time to come to terms with the idea. He'd moved to the country with her. He still lived there to be near the children. He looked after them every weekend and didn't let them down. I could tell he took his role as a father seriously.

"It felt like we'd known each other for years, it was so comfortable and easy. You know how difficult it is to get to know people who are closed. He was so different. I could tell he really loved his friends and his family. He was bright and creative and open. It felt comfortable and yet there was that incredible tension of falling in love.

"When we came to say goodbye he said, *Well, er, I really like you.* He got hold of my head and pulled me towards him and kissed me. It was almost violent. No frosty peck on the cheek.

"*Let's see each other soon. Bye!* I turned on my heels and legged it. I was so excited. I had to see him again. Halfway down the street I got out my mobile and started jabbering to my friend: *Oh my God, I've met someone really lovely and I really fancy him!*"

Second meeting

"It was a very hot night. There'd been a bad storm. All the roads were closed due to flooding. I was driving. I kept pulling over, getting text messages from him. The pub where we were going to meet was closed because it was flooded. I parked at the side of the road not too far from the Serpentine, and got out of the car. It felt like Miami, a really foggy hot summer evening. I saw him. He just ran across the road, picked me up and hugged me close, so physical and open, it was quite exhilarating. He knew he really wanted me.

"We went to a programme of short films at the summer pavilion. Endless films about windows and trees. The pavilion had no sides—you could see headlights in the mist. Matthew whispered: *Do you think what links all these films is that they're the most boring films ever made?* I guess they were beautiful but we weren't in the mood. So we went off to a pub in Pimlico. I was driving. He was quiet. I wondered if he was bored, but he wasn't.

"When he had to get his train home, he said: *I really like you.*

"I said: *I really like you too.*

"He said, *No, I really really really like you.*

"We kissed in the street. We couldn't stop. It felt teenage. At last he said: *We could continue this. Why don't you just drive me home?!* It was nearly too intense."

Third meeting

"Noah was with the childminder. Matthew came over. The tension was almost intolerable. I just had to have him stay with me. He said it felt like he'd been my husband for thirty years—in the nicest possible way.

"He said: *Is it too early to ask you to marry me?*

"I said: *Is it too early to accept?*

"We were both deadly serious!"

Parting

"And then I was away for a month in New York, after we'd only slept together a couple of times. What torture that was. He wrote some beautiful love letters across the Atlantic, but it was scary because we both thought it might all be an illusion and we might not like each other when we next met."

Meeting

"For Matthew's birthday we went to his parents' home. Meeting them was such a relief. They both hugged and kissed me. His dad's a vicar. Straightaway he said: *You're jolly brave, Arden, the whole family's here. This must be very difficult for you meeting us all at once. Do you want a stiff drink?*

"After lunch the kids were playing together, eight of them in all, it was lovely, and I was so relaxed I fell asleep—unthinkable with my previous in-laws. And you know those curtains in the photo? They were his mum's. They belonged in a twelfth-century vicarage!"

Charted waters

"A lot of our relationship has been conducted through post-it notes. He always leaves me a message on the mirror in the morning. Often they're cartoons. Like a drawing of a glass and a little speck next to it, and the words: *WATER, GRAIN = PURE LOVE*. He's very romantic. It would be sad if he wasn't romantic—he was born on Valentine's Day.

"So for Valentine's Day, his birthday, he made me a cake—a huge chocolate layered heart. It was gorgeous. He stuck little pieces of wire into it with post-it notes on each one like flags.

YOU MADE

MY

HEART

BLOSSOM

"And I made him something. I found this old 1950s map of the seas around Finland. It's as big as a dinner table. Lovely heavy paper and tons of little numbers and tiny islands and swirling currents and words with Finnish accents. I wrote names about different moments of our relationship and printed them out on tissue paper. They're not all happy.

We've already had some turbulent times with two households, and kids, and drawing boundaries with ex-partners … I made the names look like Finnish, long words run together, sprinkled with dotted accents. I stuck them all over the sea currents so that they blended with the background. It's nearly all water. Matthew has the map on his wall. And all the other bits and pieces, souvenirs of precious moments, he keeps in a trunk like an old treasure chest.

"Even if it doesn't work out with Matthew, I know he won't just give up. And I'll have regained my trust."

MÄP ÖF LÖVE (TÖ DÄTE)
Bäyöfdöubt
Pöst-itnötciceshelf
Peskykidsfjörd
Völcänösöfmutuälinstäntätträctiön
Wäshingupmöuntäin
Öpenäircinemäärchipelägö
GULFÖFÖVERWHELMINGLÖVE
Pöwell&Pressburgericeflöes
Uncömförtäblethreeweekäbsencechännel
Bäggägecöve
Häppinesssträits
Römänweekendöceän
Häppychristmäsisles
Curzöncäfcvälley
Guärdiänsöulmätestrench
Detöxtundrä
Wickwärbirthdäysäturdäyridge
Böundäriesböulders
CÄPEÖFHIGHHÖPES

The closure of a couplet

~ ❦ ~

David leaned over his work. He adjusted his glasses, cleared his throat and began to read. He had a good, deep, rich voice. Younger than the shock of his white hair.

Oh, it was you. Through winter's long enclenching
Yours was the hard bud on the frosted bough
And it was you beneath the rain's harsh drenching
Sliced the black earth with your steel bladed bough.

His first sonnet was not written for a mysterious muse or mistress, but for a psychoanalyst, in gratitude. It was a revelation of himself, he realized as he read it, hearing his hard bud words from his audience's angle. He looked up at the group. This was the poetry class he'd joined, fresh into his retirement. They were listening attentively, each one as idiosyncratic in listening as in writing. One poet leaning forward like a hungry crow. One with his eyes closed and dreaming. One stroking her fingernails in a quiet fidget. Another gripping her book and staring at its blank cover.

David continued.

You are the one who under summer's thunder
Thrust the seed deep under the thick, wet soil,
You are the one who as the cold storms plunder
The ruins of hedges sense the fruit of your toil

Splitting like teeth that would suck, thrusting a
shoot like a tongue
Hungering for the rain's love, and through the
stony earth
Sinking its root like conviction, like safety, rung
Upon rung building down the slow steps of the hearth.

One of the other poets was staring at David's shoes. She had big bright eyes, startled hair. It was just conceivable that she was enjoying the poem but not the shoes. He finished with his last two lines.

This the winter's amaze. This the shock when at stark
Cold's barest, green abruptly embroiders the dark.

It was satisfying, the sonnet's form. The pure geometry of it, three stanzas of four lines, alternating rhymes, the closure of the couplet. David liked that. Stark and dark. Two properly ended words enclenched by consonants crisp as sticks.

After the class, Vicci chatted with him, despite his footwear. Her poetry was dramatic, extreme, full of internal rhymes. The intensity of her content affected her form. She broke her sentences, snapped them into pieces, left them lingering over one stanza to another.

Vicci liked his sonnet. She responded to it in emotional ways David had not imagined. Everyone sloped off for a drink together. Gin and tonic. They continued the class after the class. Analysing phrasing, parsing, pacing. It became a habit. They were a society of poets. And when the course was over, they decided to carry on the society. For years, never mind terms.

It was five years after the sonnet that David broke up with his partner. He had been with her for twelve years. His marriage before that had lasted thirteen. They were still friends, agreeing that a rancorous settlement would be no good for the children.

It was six years after the sonnet that David bought a house in London, founded a poetry magazine and asked Vicci out for a day.

They went to Uffington in the Wiltshire Downs, a bucolic backdrop for two poets in love with nature, wine and food. They walked to the white horse, a giant four-legged Bronze Age beast cut into shallow upper slopes—easily seen from a god's eye view, but hard to see entirely, clearly, close up. Optical stimulated luminescence dating had given the horse its three thousand years by testing how long the loam had been hidden from sunlight. Dark and stark. Pagan Vicci believed in the pre-Christian spirit destroyed by dogmatic religion. Agnostic David believed that paganism was mostly a nineteenth-century invention. Vicci produced the perfect picnic. She seemed keen. David thought she was intense, almost melodramatic. He didn't want to follow it up. He let it hang, like one of her verses, even though they saw each other at the poetry group and at meetings for the magazine. He was, in fact, rather taken with another woman.

I lead a life of severe self-control mitigated by moments of impulse, wrote David in his diary, explaining to himself why it was that he'd suddenly asked Vicci to come away with him for a weekend. All sorts of issues arose now. What would this weekend imply? Everything had consequences, actions, reactions. What about the hard question of beds? He solved the problem by avoiding it.

"Do you mind if I fix the transport and you fix the hotel?" he asked her.

She called back later. "I can't get two singles. Do you mind a double room?"

His car broke down, so the weekend became five days. They shared a bed, their bodies rhyming, in a hotel on the eastern flank of the Black Mountains. They both loved walking, talking, country, poetry. David noticed that Vicci was extremely beautiful. She was elegant and smart. He hadn't thought about her in that way before. They almost felt like the perfect couplet. They returned to London, to their separate homes.

How to make my mark when standing naked,
Salt-encrusted, out of the sea.
I've survived, I'm back,
I respect my adroitness,
But
My head suddenly aches with shaking seas

David cherished his independence. He was seventy-one. Vicci was twenty years younger. They had different friends, a different social life. They would sleep together, then he'd go home. He liked being alone. The relationship dwindled, both dissatisfied, until she dumped him. She put it in writing. He replied with a well-argued letter as to why she shouldn't quit.

He didn't write poems about her. He wrote about other things. His granddaughter. German history. Birds, buds and trees.

That unsettling scent
like a woman who catches up with you in the street
and then walks on.

He felt that curious mixture of sorrow and relief that marks each end as a new beginning. He started to go out with other people. Widows, adventurers, sex, no sex, nothing particularly satisfactory.

He continued to write poetry, remembered how he'd first discovered it. He'd taken a book off his father's library shelf. At twelve years old, he'd marvelled at the cadence and lilt of Lyly:

Cupid and my Campaspe played
At cards for kisses; Cupid paid.

He sent Vicci a non-committal Christmas card, nice and early. She had time to reply; she did. She responded with the usual season's greetings, no more. He set about writing her another of his cogent crafted letters, about why they should be with each other.

It didn't work.

He missed her. They were natural together. She was bright, creative. She didn't bore him. He mused and rused.

I have been told that the emotions of old men
die down. I have not found it so, but rather
they are distilling into pure desire—

Vicci had a friend. He would consult her for advice, if only he knew how to contact her. He wrote a message. Brief. He knew the terrace where she lived, checked every single doorbell to find the name, pushed his letter in.

I'd like to talk to you about Vicci. I need some advice. Give me a ring. Please.

"I feel I've messed it up with her," he confessed in person. "I don't know how I can get her back and fix things."

The friend's words were simple. "Why don't you just tell her how you feel?"

David hadn't thought of that. He'd been too busy composing arguments.

He wrote a different kind of letter.

Vicci met him again over food and wine. Fish.

He told her how he felt.

Flip, flounder, gleam.

He asked her to move in with him not long after. She kept her flat, just in case—it helped her to take the plunge from full-time employment to freelance. They started to live together, and soon they were both working from home, sharing the same spaces by day and by night. They took turns at cooking for each other. She had always lived on her own, so the simple pleasures of domestic life gave her new satisfaction. She was good-hearted. She didn't bear grudges. He became more caring, less demanding, as a consequence of loving her.

They broached the subject of marriage.

She proposed a stone circle, just the two of them, man and wife.

He proposed a big party for all their friends.

They decided on a venue, Kew Gardens, a botanic backdrop for two poets in love with nature, wine and food. They agreed on a civil ceremony, a champagne tea.

He wanted to be married, but with a degree of apprehension. It was about the finality of commitment. There was a sense of loss for him as well as gain. He felt compelled to consider once again his space and independence. The closure of options, how he liked being alone. The closure of coupling, how he liked being with her.

Secretly, we each thought we were getting married for the other's sake. Now we're both tickled by that.

Not so secretly, she wrote a poem to read out on their wedding day.

Villanelle for my Valentine

Old love, I thought I'd never see the time—
because of all we've done and often said—
when I'd be yours, my dear, and you'd be mine.

And what relief to soften, and resign
the battle of the heart over the head.
Old love, I thought I'd never see the time

when qualms and cold feet that could undermine
all we've held out for, dissipate instead
now that I'm yours, my dear and you are mine.

I'm still amazed how our two lives align—
the two of us! A pair! Take it as read,
old love, I thought I'd never see the time.

The tangle of our jumpers on the line,
the battle for the blankets in our bed
confirm that I am yours, and you are mine.

So then, this is my pledge, my Valentine:
my hand's in yours for all that lies ahead.
Oh love, there's never been a better time
now that I'm yours, and finally, you're mine.

M
15

New York, London V

~ ❦ ~

Marcus,

Hello, friend. I haven't heard from you in a while. I hope all is well and that you're enjoying the summer. How warm can it get over there?

I'm still waiting tables, much to my chagrin. I also have to find a new apartment because I can no longer afford rent here. My roommate's mother, I may have mentioned, owns the place and has raised the rent in order to make a profit because she's financially strapped. Aren't we all? So that's at the top of my agenda. I'll make you aware of my forwarding address when I get one.

Otherwise I'm reading, composing a bit on my mom's piano (when I get over there), working and enjoying Central Park in this summer weather.

A dear friend, a phenomenal drummer and all-around great musician has been presenting some jingles to HBO and has asked me to collaborate with him. If the tunes get picked up I could stand to earn a few thousand bucks! And of course that means an eventual trip to Europe, with England as a definite destination. How could I diss my friend Marcus?

But that won't be for a while, unfortunately. Decide on an NYC trip yet? I must seem like a royal pain-in-the-ass, huh? I think I ask you that in every letter I send you. It's just that come August or September—I can't recall exactly when—it will be a year since you and I met. Wow. Impressive that we've been so dedicated to our correspondence.

Although you've been quite a slacker as of late. I remember a few months ago when I didn't write for about 6 weeks. I guess it's payback time, huh?

I'm sure you're busy.

I wish I could say I was.

Actually, I'm a bit lonely. Don't get me wrong, generally I'm in perfectly good spirits (I'm not a mood-swing kind of girl). It's just that I long for companionship lately. I don't date, as I'm sure I've stated to you, so meeting guys only happens in the workplace, and they're either gay or real players who just want to get laid (which I don't fall for). When a guy asks for my number, I DO NOT GIVE IT—EVER. I don't know why I'm telling you all this again. It's actually a bit embarrassing.

I tend to repeat myself.

I tend to repeat …

… alright, I'll stop.

Perhaps it's because you and I met and we seemed to get along so well and our letters are so packed full of personality and I await those letters with such excitement that I suppose I'm frustrated that I can't get to know you better. It just seems that in my life so many RIGHT things have slipped through my fingers.

I'm a good person. I live life according to a set of standards based on right and wrong, treating others as I would want to be treated ('The Golden Rule' is basically my religion), and yet I'm alone. My piano teacher says we live alone after we're born alone and then we die alone. Yes, we're all truly alone—we're the only ones inside our heads eating, breathing, making decisions and carrying them out—but I know so many people who have certain things that they don't appreciate, like money, a great lover, friends, shelter, a good job, etc. I have so much love inside me and sometimes I feel I'm about to burst, because there's no one here to give it to! I'm not husband-shopping, by any means. My sisters have made attempts to set me up with guys they think I'd be intrigued by, but I found them appalling and was actually insulted that they thought I'd like these losers. And a couple of them were lawyers!

I'm going to be very open and tell you that I'm fairly disappointed you live overseas because you are someone I would've given my number to—in fact, I think I did! That's saying a lot! But you probably have a girlfriend now and don't know how to tell me, and that's why you haven't written …

If you're seeing someone, that's wonderful. I hope she's lovely. We're friends, first and foremost. Just keep writing.

Now it's your turn, Mr London. I look forward to hearing from you, and think of you often. Your picture, incidentally, still hangs in the side cracks of a framed mirror in my room. What did you do with mine?

Also, refresh my memory and tell me how we first

met, or how we first struck up conversation with each other. Did we meet in the line at the jazz show? Or was it inside? Just wondering …

Take care. I hope you're having lovely weather and enjoying it. Bye!

Lots of love
Michèle
XOXO

Dear Michèle,

I've just received your letter—walked out of my house, bought a notepad and wandered down to my favourite tapas bar (with your letter to read it again in a moment), ordered a large espresso and sat down.

First, you've not been far from my mind over the last couple of months (although I haven't written). I don't think I've found myself in the right frame of mind to write in a meaningful way from <u>me</u>—I think it would have been kind of distant, which didn't really seem worth doing as we are distant geographically anyhow! This is also to do with my having been very busy at work and socially—but more importantly I have got a long way from what I've been <u>feeling</u>. Your letter arrived after a heavy 'partying' weekend, and it really touched me. It brought me back to considering the most important things—not stupid drunk and druggy conversations where nothing of you is given, and pretending that it's all cool cos hedonism is very rock and roll … Wo—stop.

As I walked down here I had composed a whole letter to you in my head—which is not coming out as clearly on paper—and now my Spanish sardines have arrived, which look great—perhaps I'll stop to eat for a second and slow down a little.

I managed not to get olive oil all over this!

I really hope you get the work with the producer—is it promising? You must get <u>that</u> voice out to as many people as possible. I find it frustrating that you are across that ocean—I'd love to get into a studio with you *and sort out some big tunes! Maybe my stuff would be a little too electronic/dancey for you—I dunno—but I could at least try and win you round!*

Your letter really struck a chord with me when you wrote about your feelings at the moment. I think I told you before that my previous relationship was in its last days some time ago now. I've kind of seen other people over the last year, but never to any length of time and not really in any sort of 'relationship' sense. I am inherently independent but/and, like you, someone must excite me as a companion before I'm interested in anything more. I've not found that for a long time now and I get more and more fussy. It is strange, however, that the more careful, independent and choosy you are, the more attractive you seem to become to all the wrong people! I hope that doesn't sound arrogant. I saw 'American Gigolo' last night—it's a fairly average film and so 1980s—but I guess it's about the same stuff—hedonism, pleasure, success all based on such unsteady ground both materially and emotionally—you have to keep searching to see where you are.

I too am disappointed you live across the ocean. I love your letters. I appreciate so much the purity of our communication without social pressure or judgement from anyone outside—totally personal between only you and me, and although we are sometimes politely tentative, we both break out at times and really express ourselves.

We met properly in the club! We started chatting by the bar—there were a few people around—you had been talking with someone who I could sense rather liked you. You told me about your origins and culturally mixed family—you talked with gusto and energy—you were guarded, as someone who is used to the attentions of men and knows how to handle it, but not to the degree of being aloof. You stood close to me as you talked, which I liked. You didn't dance to start with, but then we did—in fact, we sort of danced but then just carried on chatting on the dance floor, leaning against a pillar! The music was quite laid back.

We decided to go on to another club—you disappeared to find some money and then came back—slowly walking down the street with a white jumper over your shoulders—we got a cab to the club and the others weren't there—you looked a bit concerned! You didn't really know me, did you!? We danced, more fully this time—the others arrived and we sat upstairs chatting again. We talked about a lot of stuff but I don't remember it specifically. I found you attractive but I wasn't talking to you with ulterior purpose—I don't think we were particularly flirtatious—just interested and communicative.

We've been writing now for some 10 months or so. I was going to phone you actually the day after just to say thanks for a good night but decided to write instead. I've thought of phoning you since—I keep forgetting the time differences! If you're feeling like a chat any time do call me—I'd call you back.

A good friend is going to New York this weekend. He invited me to come. I actually got as close as going to the travel agents and reserving a seat last week, not really expecting to go—I can't afford it at the moment.

I think, however, I'm going to reserve a flight in September when the prices come down again—one year on, maybe? I'm definitely coming to NY before the end of this year to see you. It will happen.

Your picture is on my shelf in my living room—you, that is, aged very young! I've still not got a more recent one.

I think I understand what you mean by 'lonely'—not that you haven't got people around you, friends, people to spend time with—but perhaps someone you can really get lost with and in—to whom you can turn and laugh and collapse with. I think it's wonderful that you write that you are bursting with love to give. It is a crime there is no one there to give it to …

I have spent years now trying to learn how to open myself up more to others—I think I'm improving (!) but still find it hard. It is a cliché but English people do not talk about their feelings much—find it hard to tell anyone they love them without having given it intense intellectual analysis. I think we are frightened of being sentimental—uncertain of it and perturbed by it. It is a northern European trait. I had a French girlfriend for a year or so after I left college—she used to try and get me angry to make me scream at her in order that she could see my raw emotions! Actually I lived with an Italian girl for a couple of years. Same problems! I think I am a lot better now but I used to be soooo English.

I think I'll send this to you now, Michèle.

I will not be such a "slacker" again.

I will not be such a "slacker" again.

(X 100)

Thank you again for your life-enhancing letter. Even if things are sometimes difficult there must always be good things to look forward to. Seeing you will be one of the big good things for me. Take care of yourself.

Lots of love
Marcus
XX

Dear Marcus,

You are an incredible pen pal (and friend) and I wouldn't ever want to give up what we have. And if you see me again some day and fall madly in love with me, well, then one of us may have to move overseas. Did I just make your face turn white as a sheet? Good. I meant to startle you.

I've been contemplating calling you, too, but something's been holding me back. Perhaps it's the same thing I fear in sending you a current picture of myself. I'm afraid the fantasy—the foggy images we have of each other's faces and voices (although you have my tape)—will somehow be distorted or even ruined. What if we have nothing to say?! What if we can only communicate well in letters? And loud clubs with strobe lighting!

September is less than 2 months away. I can't believe I may see you that soon. So much pressure! What if you come specifically to see me and it's a nightmare? What if I irritate the hell out of you? You'll have wasted a ton of money! I'm not dissuading you from coming. I <u>want</u> you to come. Have you figured out where you'd stay? I think you mentioned that you have a friend or two you could crash with.

When's your birthday? Well, we must have missed each other's since almost a full year has gone by and neither of us has mentioned them. Unless I've forgotten you have. Mine was a month ago and I turned 25. I won't complain to you about aging because I know how you elderly people get when you hear young people whine about it. I don't want to be insensitive.

Sarcasm …

OK. No more. I hope this note finds you happy and healthy and not overworking yourself. Take care. Thanks again for your excellent letter. I've read it 3 or 4 times.

Much love,
Michèle

PS I felt a chill crawl up my spine when I saw the '…' after your line "I think it is wonderful that you write that you are bursting with love to give. It's a crime that there is no one there to give it to …". I don't know why exactly. When I see that punctuation I feel that there's more to come.

I must retire now. This letter took a lot out of me. A lot more than the one I just tore up.

Marcus,

DON'T read this until you hear the tape! I mean it!

OK, now that you've heard the tape, you can continue reading …

… when you called me at my mother's yesterday it was the only good thing that happened all afternoon. My mother and I went to see my grandmother, which I don't enjoy. She's not a particularly pleasant woman, first of all, and second, I don't enjoy the depressive atmosphere of a room full of old, sick people. They're all so bored. I feel awful for them. My mother and I had a tiff in the car on the way back into the city.

Your call made an otherwise lousy day bearable.

Or frustrating! I couldn't stop thinking about you! It was so great to hear you talking directly to me. It had certainly been a while! It was as if I'd finally spoken to a friend I hadn't seen in ages and who I missed very much.

Wait—that's exactly what it was.

Your laugh over the phone was so much more exuberant than your laugh on your tape. Both charming, of course. I heard in your voice and your laugh a bit of nervous excitement. Forgive me for jumping to conclusions, but I can empathize, as I was experiencing the same feelings. My fear of a phone call from you has vanished, incidentally. I so enjoyed it that since yesterday I have felt an irrepressible urge to talk to you almost non-stop. I listened to your tape again (that makes 5 times) and also wrote you several letters to send you along with the tape I recorded. I re-read your letters because of this urge I have to talk to you. I got such a clear sense of who you are. Also, I've been reminded of how well you actually know me. I meant it when I said you can crash at my place (if I have one by then) if need be. I'm your friend and that's the bottom line.

I think I still owe you $20.

Will a week be enough time to get out and absorb all that we want to? I have such visions of our upcoming time together.

One of your letters ends, "If you carry on writing letters like your last one it's going to get frustrating—I want to see this girl again! What's happening, Ms Manhattan??" I'd forgotten you wrote like that, Marcus, and I felt a shudder run through me like a jolt of electricity.

Get your English ass over here …

Michèle

My sweet,

I told you this morning I was out last night with some friends in a bar near me. It's a great place—a bit like the one we went to in NY. My mind was just wandering. I think I was being very rude—people were talking to me and I was not really listening, just looking and nodding and smiling occasionally. I was thinking of so many things—how could I be with you—how I wished you were with me so you could see some of "my world"—but also whether "my world" is big enough for me at the moment, whether it is too small and unadventurous—there is so much to do and I really feel I want to experience so much with you—I'd love to travel again in Europe or across the States or in South America. You've woken me up and woken these wonderful feelings and I'm on a road.

It's now afternoon, I've finished my court work and I have come back to the office. I had a good day—got everyone out and a good sentencing decision for one kid I quite like and who I think deserved a chance rather than being in prison for the next year. I used to get such terrible feelings of guilt and worry doing this work—did I say the right thing—could I have said more—should I have said less—the consequences sometimes seemed so awful—I think I have it more in perspective now. I know when a decision is right and that probably whatever I'd said wouldn't have changed it—and if it wasn't right then I'd fight by appealing it all the way.

Sunday night
I so enjoyed our conversation this morning. I think they should just set us up a line for ourselves—just for us—that is always open and free—they should just celebrate the quality of our communication and let us talk for nothing. I'm going to see a movie tonight—I wish you could come—we should catch a movie or two next week—next week—sounds good.

Monday evening
I have spent all afternoon feeling such warmth in me towards you. You picked me up at lunchtime. I drove back to court smiling and exhilarated and so happy that I have you as a friend. If we can chat like that and laugh and flirt and make love before we go out to work when we can be together then life will be just <u>too</u> good. Michèle you just sparkle sometimes. You talk and laugh and make me <u>melt</u>. It is quite uncontrollable. I just love the sound of your voice and the way you express things, the way your voice changes from hard and pointed to gentle and more childlike—I know you do it tongue in cheek, but it just makes me laugh and makes me want to be with you and hug you and kiss you on both cheeks and then gently on your lips.

I've decided that you just have to come back with me!! Just take you to the desk at the airport when I arrive and buy a ticket there and then—then we know we'll have more than just a few days together.

Oh hell, I've got to keep real haven't I!?!

As I said today I am just looking forward to the time we <u>are</u> going to spend together. I do so enjoy this situation of *being led by my heart—it is so unusual for me—what did you write? "Where is Marcus and what have you done with him?" He's still here just discovering new things in himself rather than losing himself completely. I want you to help me show me more of myself—how terribly selfish that sounds—it wasn't supposed to—. I hope you know what I mean—you always do.*

'NYPD' just came on—I love the way they film it—it makes me slightly sick and the dialogue is just so fast—their interview techniques are enough to make me jump up and object—and they really hate lawyers—"low-life mouthpieces". In fact I shouldn't like it, but I do.

I'd better send this now, otherwise it'll arrive when I do and we couldn't have that.

Hope you like the tape—it's hard to find songs that really sum up what I feel for you. I don't think they've been written, so I'll just have to write them myself—in the meantime, these will have to do—some of them are there for their spirit rather than lyrics. The house mix is there just to show off a bit!!

Michèle, when you receive this I'll be over in a few days—I cannot wait—the days are too long at the moment—they say you shouldn't wish away life—at the moment I don't care what they say—I want it to be 3.30 on Thursday and have you in my arms.

You're wrapped all around my heart, my sweet.

I adore you and …

Marcus
XXXX

CS
WHERE
CAN'T FIND
I WAN

ARE YOU, I
OU, I LOVE YOU
T TO MARRY
YOU
COM

Just right

~ ❦ ~

Lilian is ninety-four, blonde and curly. One blue eye isn't working too well any more. The other blue eye fixes on me, bright as a button. Her face is bony and her skinny frame feels brittle as a biscuit when we hug. She is tiny, like a girl.

"Everyone is so kind to me," she says with a grin. Her whole face lights up, even her hair seems brighter with smiling.

She has moved to sheltered accommodation. The lift is smart and soundless. The corridors are clean and hung with pictures of flowers and movie stars from once upon a time. Everything is on one level, brand new, rose-pink and cream. Bright orange security cords hang from ceilings. Protective spirits can be summoned as fast as it takes to wish for them: the caretaker, the paramedic, the men in blue.

Lilian can't go too far without gasping for breath, and beyond the flat she needs to be pushed in a wheelchair. She used to smoke fifteen cigarettes a day, not one more, not one less. She had a system. Fifteen was just the right number. Ever since she was sixteen. She and her sisters used to pile out of church on a Sunday and they couldn't wait to light up. They were young and smooth-skinned, sparking with life's hope between two world wars. Lilian used to like a nice drink, as well. Gin was her favourite, but not too

much. She gave up drinking and smoking just before he
ninetieth birthday and she has never looked back. N
regrets. She's had a good life, even if she is a widow.

"I've had a good life," she says, believing it, and it comes true. Her appreciation of experience is like light inside her. She shines with it and people warm to it, feeling its irresistible attraction.

Everyone loves Lilian. Ambulance drivers, carers, grandchildren, former employers. And dear old friends like Winifred, who calls every night before going to bed.

"Wini calls and she says *Good night, Lil, sleep well, love you, we'll talk in the morning.* It's always the same words. I know it by heart."

Every night of every week of every month, Lilian goes to bed with this message of love in her mind, the last words she hears before she falls asleep. And Winifred does too, because the message is two-way. I wonder if it keeps them both young.

They used to live in two different tower blocks on the same London council estate. The lift there was not so smart: it was graffiti-proofed and scraping. When it wasn't broken down and grounded, some people used it as a toilet. The stairs were even worse.

After Lilian became ill, she couldn't manage the journey between her flat and Winifred's. It felt like a mile away. Too much strength, too many breaths. Fierce cold winds whipped up between the buildings. Slight as a child, Lilian was too easily blown over. And Winifred was frightened of using the lift. It was her fear of enclosed spaces, and heights, and danger lurking around blind corners. Like two old fairy princesses, the two friends were both trapped in their towers.

Now Lilian has moved more than a mile away, but her phone number hasn't changed, so for Winifred nothing has changed. She and she are still trapped, still connected by invisible wires.

Good night, Lil, sleep well, love you, we'll talk in the morning.

Good night, Wini, have a good night's sleep, love you, and speak to you tomorrow.

And every morning, as sure as waking up, Lilian calls Winifred. They start the day together, finding out how the other has slept, and what their plans and pains are, knowing that they are alive. Sometimes Winifred is a bit down. It's in her voice. The light is grey. Her life is in a box. She says, "Oh Lilian, it's a long day, isn't it?" And together they think of things to do. The day gets brighter.

Lilian used to work nights when she was young. She was a waitress and a barmaid. In those days everyone wore hats and gloves, there were trams in London and laws against liquor. After work Lilian used to go out drinking with two of the waiters and a French boy. I don't know what the French boy did to earn a living. He was just French.

"They didn't maul me or anything," Lilian says with sincere affection.

Just as well, because she was saving herself for marriage. They'd see her safely to her door, kiss her innocently goodnight, and they never once asked to come inside.

"They didn't expect any more than friendship. We were good friends, that's all."

And they loved Lil so much, they didn't want anyone else to join them. She'd proposed the idea of another girl (just because), or maybe two more girls to even up the numbers, but they weren't interested. They didn't need anyone else because she was the one. She was their golden girl. They were pals. They'd meet at the coffee stall on Regent Street corner, right in the middle of the West End. The big expensive shops were all closed, their dark windows shuttered or gleaming. Three boys, one blonde girl. Safe together, and happy. Their impatient breath made steam in the black shiny night. Their cigarettes made blue clouds and magic circles and silent snakes of smoke under the street lamps. They would decide where to go from there: Baker Street, Soho, Piccadilly … They were regulars, and everyone knew them, Lilian and her boys.

One night their drinking club was raided by the police. The front doors were locked. Things broke and flew in panic. They were trapped. The drinkers who got caught would have their names printed in a blacklist in the next day's papers—which was a public shame, and no place for a well-brought-up lady's name.

"Quick!" said one of Lil's boys, grabbing her arm.

They escaped to a tiny back room. The window was so high Lilian couldn't reach. One pal helped her up, and another was outside waiting to catch her. She let down her golden hair. She landed in his arms and couldn't stop laughing. There was already a cab waiting at the end of the lane. It was an ordinary London cab, not a coach and horses. But the boys had between them a bottle of whisky, a bottle of gin, a great siphon of soda and a huge bag of sandwiches. They fell into the cab together. They had a banquet and a ball, laughing at their good luck. There was trouble all across Europe, creeping closer and closer. Britain was not yet at war. London was still London, unbroken by bombs.

When Lilian was older, she worked as a housekeeper for a string of bachelors who danced across chair backs in her honour or filled huge dining tables with chocolates and flowers for her birthday. One of them took her to Brighton and offered her whatever she wanted from his antique store. But Lilian didn't wish for things. She still doesn't wish for things at ninety-four years old. Her fairy godmother has been unemployed for ever.

Another of her bachelor bosses left her an exquisite vintage oil painting, a silky portrait of an exotic girl in a reverie. (One district nurse had to be relocated because she'd shown an unhealthy interest in this artwork.) Today the dreaming odalisque sits above the wheezing Lilian on her chocolate-brown velveteen sofa. They both sit, but they both seem to float. There are vases of flowers and birthday cards on every shelf and table.

"Look at that lovely card," Lilian says, pointing to a pop-up paper-lace crown. The card is pinned to the wall so that it opens out like the sugar-white circlet from the top tier of a royal wedding cake.

Not long now till you get That Special Letter, her bachelor friend has written.

"What letter's that then?" Lilian asks, pretending not to know that it's six more birthdays until the Queen Herself will write with congratulations on being awake for a hundred years. Lilian doesn't mind waiting. She's had a good life and people are so kind. The printed message on the card says *Queen for a Day*, never mind princess.

But if I have to pick my fairy tale, I like to think of Lilian as a very old Goldilocks.

She'd walk into any bear's home and happily rearrange the furniture. Goodness knows how many beds she's made and closets she's cleared. She's not shy of speaking her mind. She has a place for everything and everything in its place. Her crowning glory is her hair—thick, lustrous, young, gold—although sometimes the hairdressers give it an apricot tinge.

Before the days of dyeing, Lilian was engaged no less than three times, no more.

"The first one was too soft," she says. "He was soppy! He went along with everything! I'd say what about this or what about that, and he'd always say yes. It didn't matter what I said. It was always the same answer. He gave in to everything. You can't have that in a man. I like people to stand up for themselves, don't you? They've got to have their own opinion, know their own mind. I could tell it was going to go nowhere. I couldn't marry him. We weren't right for each other."

When she called the engagement off, he was baffled and broken. He cried like a boy and asked how he'd wronged her. But he hadn't done anything wrong; he just wasn't the right one.

The second fiancé pestered and pestered her. "I want to marry you," he always used to say, at work, on the street, in the middle of things. He was very determined. They both worked in the same bar. They went out together for a while.

"But he was too much the other way! Too hard, too demanding, too headstrong. He always wanted his own way—he stole things too—you can't have that in a man."

Then there was Gilbert and he was just right.

The first thing Lilian knew about Gilbert was from his father. He was having a drink at the bar where she was working.

"My son would really like you," he said. "I'm sure you'd get on."

Lilian was not so sure. He seemed like a gentlemanly kind of fellow, but do fathers ever know their sons that well? She thought not. Her own dad, who'd fallen from riches to rags after the Wall Street Crash, was a good father, and strict, and wanted the best things for his children, but he was still a father. Her beautiful golden-haired mother was more like a friend, but do parents know their children that well?

"Do you mind if I introduce you?" Gilbert's father asked.

Lilian agreed to meet up.

She liked the son straight away. "He was just right."

Gilbert was shy at first but he had good looks. They had a drink together after work, all three, and then they went for a stroll, with Gilbert's father walking ahead. Gilbert made her laugh. They got on so well.

"I'd like to see you again," he said, as they parted. "I really like you."

And she said: "Yes, all right."

Gilbert was a barman, a steady worker. His face was kind, because he was kind through and through. He was clean and honest and orderly. Easygoing but not soppy. He stood up for things, had opinions, knew his own mind. He set her off laughing when she least expected it, caught her unawares. At work he made fancy drinks and it was a performance, crushing half lemons in the air, pouring spirits up and down and sideways like a squeezebox, juggling cocktail olives. She could see he did it for joy, not for attention. He knew how to talk but he knew how to listen. He was a real gentleman. Not the type to mess around. And he made a fuss of her, though not in a vain pretending way like some fellows. She trusted him. He wanted to marry her soon. She'd been saving herself for marriage and he was the one, he was just right, she was sure of it. They couldn't see much point in waiting. So they went to the registry office and waited outside. Only two couples at a time, that was the system.

"How was it?" another bride-in-waiting asked as one pair of newlyweds came out.

"It was easy!" laughed the wife through a shower of rice.

Lilian and Gilbert had a daughter. They adored her. He took little Gloria to Petticoat Lane market every Sunday and always bought her a toy, one thing, whatever she wanted.

"She even chose her own pram," beams Lilian.

Gloria lives over the hills and far away, but she visits Lilian every week and always brings her groceries, whatever she needs.

"She is just like her father, exactly like him, kind through and through."

One day Gilbert left Lilian to go to work and was halfway down the road. He came back. She thought he'd forgotten something. He hadn't. At the door he just said how much he loved her, how very, very much, and gave her a great big hug and a kiss before heading back to work again.

"You'll be late!" she laughed, waving him off.

But he never got to work. He died of a heart attack in Piccadilly, just fell down in the middle of the street. He never got to be old.

I know Lilian misses him, and she has lived half her life without him, but I like to think that every day she has his message of love in her mind, the very last words she heard him say.

The photographers

~ ~

Augusto Braidotti *abraidot@bigpond.net.au*

shoes (p. 18)
piazza (pp. 24–25)
escalator (pp. 26–27)
umbrella (pp. 144–145)

Assistant photographer in Milan, cocktail barman in the Alps, life-saver then hamburger-maker on the north Adriatic (the *Vitellone* phase), drifter in Paris, rustic recluse in Friuli, cultural pilgrim in America, double-migrant in Australia … One constant throughout Augusto Braidotti's life has been photography. He captures the memories that inhabit places, what people leave behind.

Rob Hann *www.robhann.com*

hope (pp. 98–99)
FF4DM (pp. 180–181)
WhereAreYou (pp. 198–199)
lost highway (pp. 208–209)
found (pp. 210–211)

Born in Salisbury, England, and raised on the family farm, Rob has been a farm labourer, watch repairer, factory worker, fireman, kitchen worker, busboy, waiter, bartender, bicycle messenger, model, bouncer, and is now a photographer. He has lived in London, Texas, Milan, Paris and New York City. He is currently photographing America and its inhabitants.

Steve Mullins *www.dodge-burn.com*

frozen (pp. 72–73)
dancing (pp. 110–111)
football (pp. 120–121)
interior (p. 139)

Steve Mullins has exhibited at art fairs and galleries in London and Paris. His photographs often combine graphic or design elements with human details, and unusual techniques from pin-hole exposures to printing directly onto metal. Contrasting the mechanical and the organic, his arresting compositions encourage viewers to think about their place in the visual landscape.

Elise Valmorbida

About the author

~ ❦ ~

Elise Valmorbida grew up Italian in Australia, but fell in love with London. Her first book *Matilde Waltzing* (Allen & Unwin) was nominated for two national literary awards. Her short stories have appeared in *New Writer* via the Ian St James Award, *Carve Magazine* and the Cyan Books anthologies *From Here to Here* and *Common Ground*. She currently runs a communications consultancy and teaches creative writing at the University of the Arts London.